NEW DIRECTIONS FOR COMMUNITY COLLEGES

Arthur M. Cohen   Florence B. Brawer
EDITOR-IN-CHIEF   *ASSOCIATE EDITOR*

R. Dean Gerdeman
PUBLICATION COORDINATOR

Next Steps for the Community College

Trudy H. Bers
Oakton Community College

Harriott D. Calhoun
Jefferson State Community College

EDITORS

D1526796

Number 117, Spring 2002

JOSSEY-BASS
A Wiley Company
www.josseybass.com

ERIC®

Clearinghouse for Community Colleges

NEXT STEPS FOR THE COMMUNITY COLLEGE
Trudy H. Bers, Harriott D. Calhoun (eds.)
New Directions for Community Colleges, no. 117
Arthur M. Cohen, Editor-in-Chief
Florence B. Brawer, Associate Editor

New Directions for Community Colleges is indexed in Current Index to Journals in Education (ERIC).

Microfilm copies of issues and articles are available in 16mm and 35mm, as well as microfiche in 105mm, through University Microfilms Inc., 300 North Zeeb Road, Ann Arbor, Michigan 48106-1346.

ISSN 0194-3081 electronic ISSN 1534-2891 ISBN 0-7879-6289-9

NEW DIRECTIONS FOR COMMUNITY COLLEGES is part of The Jossey-Bass Higher and Adult Education Series and is published quarterly by Wiley Subscription Services, Inc., a Wiley company, at Jossey-Bass, 989 Market Street, San Francisco, California 94103-1741, in association with the ERIC Clearinghouse for Community Colleges. Periodicals postage paid at San Francisco, California, and at additional mailing offices. POSTMASTER: Send address changes to New Directions for Community Colleges, Jossey-Bass, 989 Market Street, San Francisco, California 94103-1741.

SUBSCRIPTIONS cost $66.00 for individuals and $142.00 for institutions, agencies, and libraries. Prices subject to change.

THE MATERIAL in this publication is based on work sponsored wholly or in part by the Office of Educational Research and Improvement, U.S. Department of Education, under contract number ED-99-CO-0010. Its contents do not necessarily reflect the views of the Department or any other agency of the U.S. Government.

EDITORIAL CORRESPONDENCE should be sent to the Editor-in-Chief, Arthur M. Cohen, at the ERIC Clearinghouse for Community Colleges, University of California, 3051 Moore Hall, Box 951521, Los Angeles, California 90095-1521. All manuscripts receive anonymous reviews by external referees.

Cover photograph © Rene Sheret, After Image, Los Angeles, California, 1990.

CONTENTS

EDITORS' NOTES

Practitioners and researchers alike are hard-pressed to keep abreast of rapidly changing expectations for and from community colleges. Using literature and research to inform practice has many advantages. Practitioners can learn and adapt from the experiences of others, and they can develop programs and services based on information about what works and what does not. They can plan and implement activities that are sensitive to local and state environments, taking into account the political, governance, and finance issues that inevitably shape what happens. They can enhance the scholarship on community colleges by bringing to the professoriate a view from the trenches, a sense of reality and application to enhance theory. Finally, by remaining conversant with the literature, practitioners can glean insights into the future and gain perspectives on current issues and challenges that emphasize the wider reality within which colleges operate and for which students must be prepared.

The intent of this issue of *New Directions for Community Colleges* is twofold: first, to review recent research on topics of importance, highlighting consensus and contradictions in the literature, and second, to identify some critical challenges community colleges face and present practical options for meeting them that are supported by the findings in the literature. The intended audience includes community college practitioners seeking data and information about major issues affecting community colleges; new community college employees needing an overview of this sector of postsecondary education; the educators, research scholars, and graduate students undertaking serious research about community colleges; and state and federal agency and legislative staff members seeking a broader understanding of these institutions.

Chapter One, by Trudy Bers and Harriott Calhoun, presents an overview of research literature about community colleges. In Chapter Two, Barbara Townsend focuses on transfer rates as a key, although sometimes controversial, measure of transfer. She discusses the assumptions that undergird much of the transfer rate research and the complexities of transfer rate calculations. She describes several state and national approaches for measuring transfer, identifies implications for practice, and offers a number of suggestions to improve research and public understanding about transfer.

In Chapter Three, Debra Bragg discusses the changing nature of vocational education in the community college, models and strategies for organizing and delivering vocational education, implementation issues, and available evidence on program effectiveness and outcomes associated with student participation. She notes that for some vocational education approaches, for example, tech prep, little is yet known about program outcomes.

1

In Chapter Four, Betsy Oudenhoven identifies five issues related to remedial and developmental education: the ongoing debate about the appropriate educational level and sector for offering remediation, how to provide effective remediation programs for an increasingly diverse student population, the lack of consistent policies and practices in remediation, divergent views on the extent to which placement in remedial courses should be mandatory or advisory, and whether basic skills instruction should be embedded in the regular college curriculum or offered separately.

In Chapter Five, Amy Blumenthal presents five issues associated with students speaking or learning English as a second language, who comprise a significant and growing population at many community colleges. The issues Blumenthal derives from the literature are the diversity of the ESL student population and the difficulty of measuring student outcomes, the organizational structure of community college ESL programs, employment issues for and training of instructors, the newly defined Generation 1.5 population, and financial and funding concerns for ESL programs. Her discussion of Generation 1.5 is particularly important because it describes students who are just beginning to be recognized as a group with distinctive characteristics and academic difficulties.

In Chapter Six, Jeffrey Seybert discusses the assessment of student learning outcomes in six domains: general education, transfer programs, vocational and occupational education, remedial and developmental education, continuing education, and affective and noncognitive areas. He then discusses the use of assessment results and the implications of assessment for external accountability reporting and accreditation.

In Chapter Seven, Terry Williams identifies key challenges for student services units in the community college: student diversity, a renewed focus on student success, and calls to demonstrate program effectiveness. He reviews proposed solutions to address each challenge and notes that there continue to be large gaps in the literature, particularly in studies related to the need for student services staff to respond to demands that they be accountable to their stakeholders.

In Chapter Eight, Kim Gibson-Harman, Sandria Rodriguez, and Jennifer Grant Haworth identify key challenges for community colleges concerning faculty and professional staff: preparing and attracting qualified faculty, implementing the teaching and learning paradigm, helping faculty make use of current technology, and improving the status and morale of professional staff. They propose several potential solutions for each challenge.

In Chapter Nine, Cheryl Lovell and Catherine Trouth present information about different types of governance practices and patterns in today's postsecondary environment that affect community colleges and discuss the factors that influence statewide governance practices. They note that federal financial aid policies, new federal workforce development legislation, and state funding policies have important consequences for community college governance. Evolving statewide governance structures, an emphasis on seamless K–16 education, and the ever more pervasive world of technology constitute emerging governance issues.

Chapter Ten presents brief discussions of key literature in which the chapter authors cite a select number of works they believe are of particular importance. Taken together, this review of key literature constitutes a comprehensive, though not exhaustive, reference list for everyone interested in learning more about community colleges. Faculty who teach graduate courses on the community college could use this chapter as a reading list for students, and libraries seeking to audit or build a collection of publications related to community colleges can use it to guide acquisition decisions.

Collectively, these ten chapters tell us that while much is known about the community college, there is a continuing need to study the community college's organization, students, personnel, and functions. Both unanswered questions and misleading impressions remain. Conversely, the community college portrayed in the current literature is an institution that is on the leading edge of many of the issues and concerns that higher education faces as it enters the twenty-first century.

Trudy H. Bers
Harriott D. Calhoun
Editors

TRUDY H. BERS *is senior director of research, curriculum, and planning at Oakton Community College, Des Plaines, Illinois.*

HARRIOTT D. CALHOUN *is director of institutional research and information services at Jefferson State Community College, Birmingham, Alabama.*

The research literature on community colleges is varied
in nature, purpose, content, and accessibility to audiences
such as the scholarly community and practitioners.
Variations in the literature indicate an unfortunate gap
between practice and research.

Literature on Community Colleges: An Overview

Trudy H. Bers, Harriott D. Calhoun

This chapter provides an overview of the categories, types, and purposes of the literature on community colleges and the major publications germane to community college practitioners and scholars. The overview indicates a gap between perceptions in the research community and perceptions among practitioners regarding the important topics for research and publication.

Categories of Literature

The literature on community colleges falls into a variety of categories, although no standard set exists. We propose the following categories: informative and promotional research (with little or no analysis), advisory research (what "should" be done), descriptive research, and scholarly research. Categories overlap; the same research project might be reported in multiple publications, each directed to a different audience.

Informative and Promotional Research. This literature tends to be produced by single institutions or consortia, primarily to promote or gain recognition for a particular program, service, or process. Work is generally descriptive; the depth of discussion and amount of detail vary with the audience and publication. Because the intent is to present the institution in a positive light and to appeal to lay readers and practitioners, articles are often enhanced with anecdotes, quotations, and photographs. Publication outlets include magazine-like journals such as the *AACC Community College Journal*, institutional publications such as newsletters and annual reports, and press releases.

Advisory Research. This literature includes more substantive discussions of a particular issue or problem along with recommendations and advice. Publications are targeted to practitioners or policymakers. For example, *Innovation Abstracts,* published by the National Institute for Staff and Organizational Development at the University of Texas, is written by practitioners who describe successful teaching tips, program initiatives, and best practices. Embedded explicitly or implicitly in each issue is advice on successfully implementing the activity. State governing and coordinating boards often produce extensive analyses of a particular issue or problem, concluding with a series of recommendations for policies, practices, and funding. Although the tenor of these reports is usually dispassionate and objective, recommendations are often influenced by politics as much as good practice.

Descriptive Research. This literature is similar to informative and promotional literature in that both types present a description of a program, service, or process. Descriptive research devotes more space to results, and it may include a brief literature review, analyses of factors contributing to or associated with the outcomes, lessons learned as a result of the activity, and suggestions related to continuing and improving the activity.

Scholarly Research. Scholarly research involves, at least to some extent, articulating theories underlying the topic, posing and testing hypotheses, describing research methodology, reviewing the literature on previous studies, presenting data and results (quantitative or qualitative), analyzing and discussing results, and sometimes giving suggestions for future research. Scholarly research may include implications for practitioners but often does not. The immediate audience is the professoriate and graduate students.

Types of Publications and Sources

People usually assume that literature is "published" in the recognized formats of books or articles, but books and articles do not encompass the full range of literature.

Books. There are many books about community colleges. Two primary publishers have been Jossey-Bass and the American Association of Community Colleges (AACC). Information about community college research can also be found in books about postsecondary education, but such books may not be identified in searches that focus on community colleges. Valuable information and insights may be obtained from books about postsecondary education, but readers should exercise caution in assuming that books about higher education generally or four-year institutions specifically are directly applicable to community colleges.

Articles in Refereed Journals. The relative percentage of refereed journal articles written by scholars who work in community colleges compared to those who work in universities is unknown, as is the relative percentage of articles that focus on community colleges as the subject. We have observed that many articles about community colleges, particularly those in more highly regarded scholarly journals, are written by researchers in the higher education professoriate. Although such work is scholarly, community college practitioners have sometimes criticized the conceptual basis for the research and the conclusions drawn from it for not reflecting the realities of community college life.

Articles in Nonrefereed Publications. Other articles are published in nonrefereed journals, magazines, or expanded newsletters. They may be based on research but are likely to be descriptive, promotional, or admonitory pieces rather than scholarly research reports that include literature reviews, theoretical frameworks, statistical analyses, and in-depth discussions of findings.

Articles in Electronic Journals. Some existing print journals have established electronic versions, but many new journals exist solely in electronic form, and many individuals express uncertainty about their reliability and validity. This concern may not yet be warranted in the community college field, however, as we were unable to locate any totally electronic journals that specifically focus on research about community colleges.

State Agency Reports. Agency reports constitute a different but important source of research information. State boards often produce thick compilations of data about colleges, which are generally more useful as sources of raw data rather than for their analyses. Other reports are more analytical or seek to investigate a subject of particular state or regional concern. A scan of Web sites of community college governing and coordinating boards in Florida, Illinois, and California revealed these agency reports:

- From Florida, a report from 1996–97 summarizing how well Florida is doing with articulation among public schools, community colleges, and state universities.
- From Illinois, a FY2000 accountability and productivity report summarizing colleges' program reviews and self-reports on focused questions posed by the Illinois Community College Board or the Illinois Board of Higher Education.
- From California, a 1999 report on the effectiveness of community colleges on selected performance measures.

Dissertations and Theses. Dissertations and theses are an important research outlet. The University of Michigan maintains a compilation of doctoral dissertations and abstracts. One can search the abstracts database electronically, entering search criteria that limit the search to community colleges or other topics of interest. The direct Web site for dissertation abstract searches is http://wwwlib.umi.com/dissertations/search/basic. Dissertations, though not subjected to peer review, are nevertheless held to high academic standards. They also contain extensive literature reviews that are useful sources of information.

Institutional Reports. Institutional reports may contain data compilations (for example, fact books), investigations of specific issues at the college, or reports of applied research projects. The availability of such reports, in print or electronic form, varies greatly among institutions. A scan of Web sites of several community colleges produced these typical examples:

- From Miami-Dade Community College in Florida, a report titled "How Well Do Prerequisite Courses Prepare Students for the Next Course in the Sequence?"
- From Mount Hood Community College in Oregon, the report "Institutional Effectiveness and Educational Assessment: Indicators, Criteria, and Process," an update of the college's continuing efforts in this area
- From Sinclair Community College in Ohio, a report of results of the college's 1999 former student survey

Institutional reports are not subjected to peer or other reviews to determine quality; consequently, their utility, including the validity and reliability of the information they contain, must be judged by the reader.

Conference Presentations. Conference presentations include handouts, slides, and audiotapes as well as papers. Like institutional reports, conference presentations vary greatly in quality, depth of research reported, and adherence to commonly accepted standards for research. Obtaining materials from conference presentations is not simple unless one actually attends the conference. Sometimes a full paper or report may be available after the conference from the presenters or posted on the organization's Web site.

Proprietary Studies. Proprietary studies are projects executed at the request of a client, often by research suppliers working under contract. What distinguishes proprietary studies is that results are made available directly to the client, with no expectation that a wider audience will have access to them. The research supplier considers the research the property of the client and makes it available only to the extent the client deems appropriate.

Fugitive Literature. Many institutional reports, conference presentations, and proprietary studies fall into a broad, informal category known as fugitive literature. This literature is difficult to locate through normal search processes because the works remain officially unpublished. Often the author or institution does not choose to make them widely accessible. These works are consequently not listed in reference indexes or among resources such as ERIC documents. Expanded electronic capabilities may be easing the process of identifying, locating, and acquiring fugitive literature, particularly as institutions put links to institutional studies on their Web sites.

Purposes of Research Literature on Community Colleges

Research literature has many purposes, and the literature appropriate for one purpose or audience may not satisfy another purpose or audience.

Promotion or Visibility. One purpose not usually considered under the rubric of "research" literature is that of promoting or gaining visibility for a college project. This purpose is served by the informative and promotional category, with the emphasis on promotion. Formal research findings are given little, if any, attention in this literature, except as overall results cast the institution in a positive light.

Accountability. A second purpose of the research literature is accountability. The accountability emphasis that swept the nation in the past few years generated numerous mandated reports for state agencies, accrediting bodies, and other entities. Substantive data and information about colleges, including quantitative indicators of quality and tabulations about participation and costs, are often embedded in the reports. Accountability literature rarely contains such information as theoretical frameworks, multivariate statistical analyses, literature reviews, or implications for further research. Accountability literature resides primarily in the filing cabinets of recipient bodies and institutions submitting their reports. Performance-based funding reports, formative and summative reports to grant providers, and accreditation self-studies are examples of accountability literature.

Utility. A third purpose of research literature is utilitarian—what is sometimes called "action research." The intent of these works is to spur action: to give readers adequate information so they can begin or adapt a similar program or lobby for a particular policy or funding stream.

Generation and Dissemination of New Knowledge. The last primary purpose of research literature is scholarly, to generate and disseminate new knowledge about the subject. This body of literature is intended primarily for the professoriate, graduate students, and individuals whose primary or sole responsibility is research. Though information for practitioners may be included, the writing style and presentation format are typically formal and often full of disciplinary jargon. Practitioners may lack the disciplinary background or patience to extricate findings or ideas that will be useful. For utility in the "real world," scholarly literature needs to be "translated" into more readable forms.

The Gap Between Practitioners and Scholars

Subjects chosen for investigation by scholars seeking to publish for tenure and promotion may reflect what the professoriate and scholarly community view as important topics or characteristics of community colleges, but their choices may be different from those that practitioners or policymakers believe are most important. For example, recently much national and state attention has been paid to workforce development, remedial education, distance education, and the use of technology. Millions of dollars have been invested in training and workforce development projects and in distance education initiatives. However, systematic research on the real impact of workforce development projects and distance education continues to be in short supply.

The basic point is that research topics valued by individuals associated with universities may be quite distinct from research topics centered on contemporary community college issues or on a loosely defined "national agenda" for community colleges. This gap in perception may help explain the paucity of substantive studies about selected topics such as workforce development. Also, there may be a more fundamental gap between practitioners and scholars such that they do not effectively inform one another's work.

Not only do university faculty and graduate students choose different topics for study than community college practitioners do, but they also write for different audiences. Consequently, the research of the two groups appears in different types of publications. Much of the research conducted by community college employees is published only in institutional reports, the fugitive literature on community colleges. After producing a report for the institutional purpose for which the research was undertaken, the community college researchers have almost no incentives, other than intrinsic interest, to produce a manuscript for presentation in scholarly venues. Conversely, the works of research scholars typically published in books and refereed journals may be so theoretical and weighted with methodological detail that practitioners have little interest or patience in sifting through them for findings that might inform decisions and practice. Further, these scholars may lack both the frame of reference and the incentives to translate their work for more practical applications.

A related concern is that the individuals who review manuscripts for publication may lack experiences that enable them to accurately assess the quality of research in the community college context. If those who research and write *about* community colleges and those who research and write *within* community colleges are to benefit from each other's work, both sides must take purposive steps to bridge the gap between their interests and concerns.

Community College and Higher Education Research Publications

This section provides a brief description of major community college and higher education research journals. It does not include journals that target particular disciplines or functional areas, such as community college English or mathematics, student services, or business affairs.

- *Assessment Update* usually includes one or more articles based on community college work. The publication contains brief descriptions of all sorts of student outcomes assessment approaches, policies, and instruments.

- The *Community College Journal* is published by the American Association of Community Colleges. It contains general articles that are usually descriptive.
- *Change* magazine, published by the American Association for Higher Education, often contains articles that present research findings from studies of higher education.
- The *Community College Journal of Research and Practice* is sponsored by the Bill J. Priest Center for Community College Education at the University of North Texas in association with several other institutions. Articles are generally research-based, with reviews of books or subjects of interest also accepted.
- The *Community College Review* is published by the Department of Adult and Community College Education at North Carolina State University. Articles are based on research or experiences in community college education.
- *Community College Week* is an electronic newspaper that covers state and national news affecting community, technical, and junior colleges. The URL is http://www.CCWeek.com.
- *Innovation Abstracts* is produced by the National Institute for Staff and Organizational Development at the University of Texas College of Education, and each abstract is written by a community college practitioner. Though not a research publication, some issues of *Abstracts* contain "findings" from the practice described.
- The *Journal of Applied Research in the Community College* is the journal of the National Council for Research and Planning, an AACC-affiliate council. Its focus is on applied research that has utility for decision making and administration.
- The *Journal of Higher Education* is published by Ohio State University. It provides an array of quantitative and qualitative articles about topics in higher education.
- *New Directions for Community Colleges* is issued quarterly as part of the Jossey-Bass series of *New Directions* publications. Each issue covers a specific subject, is prepared by one or more guest editors, and is focused on practical implications.
- *Research in Higher Education* is the journal of the Association for Institutional Research. Though not focused specifically on community colleges, a number of articles report research about community colleges. The journal emphasizes empirical research that has practical implications for institutional research and decision making.
- The *Review of Higher Education* is the official journal of the Association for the Study of Higher Education. The *Review* includes a variety of articles, including review essays, about topics in higher education.

The ERIC Clearinghouse for Community Colleges is not a publication but is nevertheless a valuable resource. It is one of sixteen ERIC clearinghouses responsible for acquiring, selecting, and abstracting materials in its subject area and making them available in print or on-line. Authors submit their documents to ERIC, which has the right to accept or reject them. Be aware that ERIC standards are not as stringent as the peer reviews used to screen, revise, and accept articles published in refereed journals.

Conclusion

Although a substantial body of literature on community colleges exists, it varies in nature, purpose, content, and accessibility. University faculty and graduate students have strong incentives to conduct formal, scholarly research and to seek every opportunity for publication of their work in order to advance their educational and professional status. Practitioners in the community college do applied research to solve practical problems that relate to the operations of their colleges, but they have few incentives to produce formal research reports or to submit them for publication. To strengthen the extent to which research informs practice and to which practice is rigorously evaluated and reported, it behooves both practitioners and scholars to improve the preparation and dissemination of good research about community colleges.

TRUDY H. BERS is senior director of research, curriculum, and planning at Oakton Community College, Des Plaines, Illinois.

HARRIOTT D. CALHOUN is director of institutional research and information services at Jefferson State Community College, Birmingham, Alabama.

2

Studies of transfer rates typically yield inaccurate perceptions about the role community colleges play in baccalaureate attainment.

Transfer Rates: A Problematic Criterion for Measuring the Community College

Barbara K. Townsend

Much like Chicken Little, who ran around crying, "The sky is falling! The sky is falling!" some community college critics shriek, "Transfer rates are falling! Transfer rates are falling!" Their cries potentially alarm others into thinking the community college's transfer function is in dire trouble because transfer rates are lower than at some previous time in the two-year college's history.

Unlike Chicken Little's cries, those about falling transfer rates have some truth, depending on *how the transfer rate is calculated* and on *what time period is studied*. Most transfer rate studies focus on a particular set of transfer students: those who begin their higher education in a community college and transfer to a four-year college. Sometimes the focus is even narrower—students in a transfer or academic associate degree program or students who completed an associate of arts (A.A.) degree. The sources cited later in this chapter indicate that when transfer rates are calculated only on students who began at the community college in a transfer program and completed an associate degree, transfer rates did indeed decline in the 1980s.

In spite of some people's cries about falling transfer rates, transfer education is alive and well in the community college, and many students transfer community college credits to four-year colleges. To support this thesis, this chapter will indicate what is problematic about concerns regarding transfer rates and provide implications for institutional leaders, policymakers, and researchers.

NEW DIRECTIONS FOR COMMUNITY COLLEGES, no. 117, Spring 2002 © Wiley Periodicals, Inc.

Common Concerns About the Transfer Rate

In his New Expeditions Issues Paper on the mission of community colleges, Nora (2000) claimed that "there has been a notable decline in the percentage of community college students who transfer to senior institutions over the last 25 years" (p. 3). As evidence, he cited information derived from Friedlander (1980): "In 1973, less than 43 percent of students in two-year colleges were participating in transfer programs, and by 1980, the proportion had dropped to nearly 30 percent" (p. 3). Three other works were referenced (Dougherty, 1992; Nora and Rendon, 1998; Tinto, 1998) to substantiate his next and only other piece of supporting evidence: "Today, estimates of students who transfer from community college to four-year institutions are at about 15 to 20 percent" (Nora, 2000, p. 3). Nora did not indicate whether the 15 to 20 percent who transferred were from all students in transfer programs or from all students who enroll in the community college.

A few years before Nora's paper, Dougherty (1994) also noted "the sharp decline in the community college's role in baccalaureate preparation over the last 20 years" (p. 5). To support this statement, he cited Grubb's analysis (1991) of national transfer rates as well as data about transfer rates in California, New York, and Florida. In a footnote to another chapter, Dougherty did indicate the difficulty of accurately determining transfer rates because researchers use different definitions of transfer students. Using national data from the High School and Beyond Study focusing on the high school class of 1980, Grubb (1991) estimated a transfer rate of 20.2 percent for 1980 high school graduates. However, Grubb looked only at high school graduates who enrolled in the community college right after high school. As Dougherty noted, this approach "ignores the two-thirds of community college entrants who delay entry to college" (1994, p. 295). After citing 1980s data from Maryland, Texas, and California studies and referencing the work of the Transfer Assembly Project of the Center for the Study of Community Colleges, Dougherty chose to be "prudent." He "set the 'true' transfer rate within four years of entrance for all community college entrants (irrespective of program and aspirations) at 15% to 20%" (p. 296).

Assumptions Underlying Discussions of Transfer Rates

There seems to be a basic assumption that declining transfer rates are a problem. When falling transfer rates are presented as a concern, the assumption seems to be that they should be at a certain level. Yet this level is not stated. So what if transfer rates declined for students in the class of 1980 as compared to the class of 1972 (Grubb, 1991)? Is there a minimum transfer rate that community colleges are expected to have to justify their transfer programs? What is the ideal transfer rate supposed to be? To my knowledge, there have not been any governmental edicts or association stances on this question. For example, the American Association of Community Colleges (AACC) does not advocate a particular transfer rate as ideal (George Boggs, president, AACC, personal communication, Feb. 1, 2000).

Another assumption in some discussions of transfer rates is illustrated in Nora's use (2000) of Friedlander's information (1980) about the decrease in the percentage of students *in transfer programs*. By using this information to back up a claim of declining transfer rates, Nora's unstated assumption is that only students in transfer programs will transfer. Therefore, an enrollment decline in transfer programs automatically equates to a decline in transfer rates.

Although this assumption may have been correct at one time, it is no longer true. Many students in nontransfer programs, also known as applied associate degree or terminal programs, intend to transfer to a four-year college, and some actually do. Using data from a national survey of over 7,500 students in ninety-five randomly selected two-year colleges, Palmer (1987) found that 26 percent of the vocational students planned to transfer to a four-year college. More than a decade later, Berkner, Horn, and Clune (2000) analyzed data from the 1995–96 Beginning Postsecondary Students Longitudinal Study and found that almost 32 percent of students in associate degree programs with majors in applied fields enrolled with the intent to transfer to a four-year institution. Grubb's national study of transfer rates (1991) revealed that many students in the High School and Beyond Study transferred to four-year colleges with vocational associate degrees: more than 23 percent of community college students from the class of 1980, compared to almost 50 percent with an academic associate degree.

Definitional Issues in Determining Transfer Rates

The major difficulty in determining transfer rates is agreeing on which students should be included. Thus to determine the percentage of students who transfer, one has to determine both the denominator, which is the number of students who could have transferred, and the numerator, the number of students who did transfer (Gelin, 1999). Researchers vary in their selection of both numerator and denominator. Regarding the denominator, "some states and colleges compare the number of transfers to total headcount, others to full-time equivalent enrollment, and still others to the number of entering high school students" (Banks, 1990, p. 47). Sometimes the comparison is to students who indicated an intent to transfer or who are in a transfer program.

The choice of numerator is equally problematic. In some studies, transfer students are defined as those who complete an A.A. degree and transfer to a four-year college (e.g., Baldwin, 1994). When receipt of the A.A. degree is a criterion for calculating transfer rates, the rates will not reflect the transfer of students who did not complete the A.A. (or any other associate degree). Many community college students are committed to transferring to a four-year college at some point but not necessarily with an associate degree. Using data from the National Longitudinal Study of the Class of 1972 and the High School and Beyond Study, Grubb (1991) found an increase in students who transferred before receiving an associate degree—from 65 percent in the class of 1972 to 73 percent in the class of 1980. Berkner, Horn, and Clune (2000) analyzed data from the 1995–96 Beginning Postsecondary Students Longitudinal Study and found that 24 percent of students who started higher education in the community college in 1995–96 intended to transfer to a four-year college before they completed an associate degree. Fully half of those actually did so.

Not all studies looking at student transfer rates use receipt of the associate degree as a criterion for inclusion. For example, in Adelman's recent examination of college attendance patterns and baccalaureate attainment (1999), he used initial entry into higher education through the community college as the criterion for determining what percentage of two-year college students transferred to the four-year sector. Using this criterion, he found a transfer rate of 26 percent.

Adelman's rate is somewhat higher than that determined by the Center for the Study of Community Colleges, which also bases its calculation of transfer rates on students who enter higher education through the community college. Since 1984, the center has conducted the National Transfer Assembly Project (NTAP), which seeks to determine a national rate of transfer from two-year to four-year colleges. To determine this rate, the project uses the following definition: "All students entering the two-year college in a given year who have no prior college experience and who complete at least 12 college credit units [at that college] within four years, divided into the number of that group who take one or more classes at an in-state, public university within four years" (Center for the Study of Community Colleges, 2001).

It is important to understand the parameters of this definition of transfer student. Like Grubb's study, only students with no prior college attendance are included. Thus students who begin at a four-year college, reverse-transfer to a two-year, and then transfer to a four-year college are not included. Unlike Grubb's work, this definition does not have the parameter that students must enter the community college upon graduation from high school. Rather, students who begin at the community college several or many years after high school are included. Another parameter is transfer to a particular type of four-year school: an in-state, public one. Students who transfer to out-of-state public institutions are not counted, nor are those who transfer to private, independent, or private, proprietary institutions, in-state or out. A third parameter is the time limit of four years. Should students meet all other parameters but transfer after four years, they are not counted.

For students who met the NTAP's definition of transfer students, the transfer rate for those who started at a community college in 1995 was 25.18 percent, compared to rates ranging from 21.2 to 23.7 percent during the years 1984–1989 (Cohen and Brawer, 1996; Center for the Study of Community Colleges, 2001). As a result of this work, there are data showing the national rate of transfer for students entering community colleges since 1984. These data illustrate that transfer rates, as defined in this project, have fluctuated only a few percentage points during this fifteen-year period, sometimes falling and sometimes rising.

The NTAP is probably the best-known effort to calculate a national transfer rate. However, another initiative to do so was the work of the National Effective Transfer Consortium (NETC), established in the late 1980s with twenty-eight institutions in thirteen states. The NETC defined transfer rate as "the number of transfers divided by the number of non-reenrolling students" (Berman, Curry, Nelson, and Weiler, 1990, p. 10). More specifically, the transfers were all students who enrolled in a four-year college in the fall semester of the year in which they had previously enrolled at the community college and completed six or more college credits. This definition is distinctive for its emphasis on an exiting cohort, students who do not reenroll at a community college in the fall semester after the spring semester in which their attendance was recorded. With this definition, transfer rates averaged approximately 25 percent (p. 14).

By counting as transfers only those who enrolled at a four-year school within a few months after enrollment at a community college, the NETC risked drastically undercounting the number of transfers, since some students may have stopped out for a year or more and then transferred. Also, including as transfer students those who had completed only six units at a two-year school meant that the students had a very limited exposure to the community college curriculum (Gelin, 1999). Thus their academic performance at the receiving institution could hardly be said to reflect either poorly or positively on their community college preparation.

A recent statewide study of transfers in Oregon also included students who might have had minimum exposure to the community college curriculum. The Oregon University System and the Oregon Department of Community Colleges and Workforce Development (2000) jointly conducted a study of transfers among their institutions. Prompted by "concerns about the viability of the student transfer process, especially as it pertained to Oregon's community college students who wished to transfer to an Oregon University System campus" (p. 1), the study used analysis of transcripts to examine the transfer of Oregon community college students to an Oregon University System institution during 1995–1999. Transfer students were defined as those people who were "enrolled one year at an Oregon community college and then . . . enrolled the next academic year at an Oregon University System campus, regardless of enrollment status or number and type of credits taken" (p. 4). Using this definition of transfer students, the report concluded that contrary to the common perception that community college transfer rates were declining, the data showed a "slight" (p. 11) increase in numbers between 1996–97 and 1998–99.

Although number and types of credits taken or degrees earned prior to transfer were not parameters for this study, the length of time between enrollment at the community college and transfer to the university was a criterion. Students who enrolled more than a year after enrollment at the community college were not counted in the transfer rate. Furthermore, in determining how many students transferred with a degree, the only degree considered was the Associate of Arts/Oregon Transfer degree.

Other Difficulties in Determining Transfer Rates

Defining transfer students is also complicated by the national growth in dual-credit programs. Dual-credit programs enable high school students to take college courses offered at their high school and simultaneously receive credit for a high school and college course. Responses to a 1997 survey of state higher education executive officers (SHEEOs) yielded an estimate of more than two hundred thousand high school students taking dual-enrollment courses in 1995–96 (Crooks, 1998). In Missouri, the 1997–98 duplicated head count enrollment was forty-one thousand, an increase of 64 percent from 1995–96 (Girardi and Stein, 2001).

Because of dual-credit enrollment, some high school graduates who have never set foot on a community college campus transfer two-year college credits to a four-year college after high school graduation. In Missouri, of the students who received dual credit from community colleges in 1995–96, almost 56 percent transferred that credit when they graduated from high school (Girardi and Stein, 2001). Technically, these students are two-year college transfer students and are counted as such in the Center for the Study of Community Colleges' determination of transfer rates (Katalin Szelényi, coordinator, 2001 Transfer Assembly Project, personal communication, May 3, 2001). Whether most studies of transfer rates have included dual-credit students is not known. A review of the other studies cited in this chapter indicated that no study specifically mentioned the transfer of dual-credit courses. However, Adelman (1999) excluded "college course taking while the student was enrolled in high school" (p. 42) in his national examination of college attendance patterns and baccalaureate attainment.

Early admission programs also exist in which high school students take college classes, sometimes during the summer and sometimes during the regular school year, for college credit. When these students matriculate at a college or university after high school graduation, they are considered on Integrated Postsecondary Education Data System (IPEDS) reports to be "first-time college." Therefore, a university would enter each such student into its data system as a "freshman, first-time student" rather than a "transfer" even though the university accepts credit earned before high school graduation. It is unlikely that these students are included in transfer rate calculations.

Apart from the definitional inconsistencies in identifying community college transfer students, there are research problems associated with tracking a cohort of students after they leave a community college to see if they transfer. Sometimes institutions don't want to commit money or time to this purpose or are reluctant to gather this information because it could be used against them if the results do not show a high transfer rate (Brawer, 1991). Community colleges that do seek this information frequently rely on student surveys for it. As with any survey, the response rate may be low, so the ability to generalize from the findings of the study is limited. Also, survey responses may be erroneous, simply because of faulty memory about grade point averages or total credits earned (Clagett and Huntington, 1994). If the research is conducted at the state system level, state systems typically include only public institutions and thus may not track the flow of students from public community colleges to private colleges within the state, let alone to colleges outside the state (Brawer, 1991).

Implications for Practice

When the transfer function is narrowly defined to mean providing transfer education only to students who enter higher education through the community college and enroll in a transfer program, it devalues or ignores other kinds of community college transfers. One kind, already mentioned, is the transfer and eventual baccalaureate attainment of undergraduate reverse transfers. Also ignored is the transfer to four-year colleges of credits earned by high school students through dual enrollment or early admission programs and by four-year college students who are concurrently enrolled at a community college.

The case for including only students who begin at the community college in any calculation of transfer rates is predicated on the belief that a fundamental mission of the community college is to provide access to higher education for students who would not normally have access. Therefore, the transfer of this group of students is what matters, and the transfer of students who began at a four-year college before taking courses at the community college or who earned college credit through dual-enrollment or early admission programs is not significant (Grubb, 1991; Lee and Frank, 1990).

Although this position is debatable, the case for including only students who complete the A.A. degree or have been in a transfer program is even less credible. Many students who pursue applied degrees are among those who needed an open door into higher education. Why should these students be discouraged from transfer and excluded from calculation of transfer rates?

Institutional leaders have choices. They can accept a narrow definition of the transfer function, join the crowd crying about falling transfer rates, and participate in the consequent community college bashing. They can stop there, or they can work to increase the transfer of students who fit within the narrow definitions used in calculations of transfer rates. For example, more funds could be poured into transfer centers and academic support services. Development efforts could focus on raising scholarships restricted to first-time college-goers in transfer programs. Leaders of area four-year colleges could be lobbied to refuse admission to any community college student seeking to transfer without an A.A. degree.

Institutional leaders can help the general public, policymakers, and four-year college faculty and administrators understand that community colleges ensure eventual baccalaureate attainment for many individuals, although not necessarily in the ways intended by the original founders of two-year colleges. Institutional leaders need to remind higher education decision makers, as well as the general public, that the original mission of two-year colleges was dramatically different from the mission of the contemporary community college. Just as the two-year college mission has changed, so has the transfer behavior of two-year college students. De los Santos and Wright (1990) spotlighted the phenomenon of students' "swirling" (p. 32) among several two- and four-year colleges, rather than moving in a linear path from one community college to one four-year college. Furthermore, baccalaureate attainment is certainly facilitated both financially and temporally for four-year college students who start their college work by taking community college courses while still in high school and who take summer courses at the community college or enroll concurrently at the two institutions.

Policymakers can improve tracking of community college transfers, however they are defined. State systems of higher education should have the capacity to develop better tracking databases for public institutions within the state, perhaps even including private institutions, in order to track graduates by type of associate degree received. For example, Missouri has recently decided to track two-year college graduates of nontransfer programs as well as those receiving the A.A. degree (Terry Barnes, assistant commissioner of Missouri Community Colleges, personal communication, Jan. 1, 2000). In so doing, Missouri will gain a fuller picture of the extent of transfer among two-year college degree recipients.

Ideally, a state tracking system would also account for other kinds of transfers, such as reverse transfers, transfers of college credits earned at community colleges by high school students participating in dual-credit or early admission programs, and transfers of credits earned at community colleges by four-year college students through concurrent enrollment or summer sessions. As Adelman (1999) and others have pointed out, students "swirl through the system" (p. ix) in a variety of attendance patterns, and these patterns need to be captured at the state level.

Institutional leaders can also commit resources to membership in the National Student Loan Clearinghouse (NSLC) so that a college's institutional researchers can use the "enrollment search" database to determine if their students transfer. Developed in the late 1990s, this database enables institutional researchers to determine which of their students has transferred, when they transferred, and to what institution they transferred (Porter, 1999).

Conclusion

Disagreements over who should be counted as transfer students and potential transfer students render it almost impossible to determine a commonly agreed national rate of students transferring from community colleges to the four-year sector. Variations in definitions include differences in the time frame for transfer, students' degree program, and number of credits upon transfer (Gelin, 1999). Determining which numerator and denominator are used in calculating percentages of transfer students is critical in understanding the actual meaning of transfer rates for a particular college or state.

To choose a particular numerator and denominator, policymakers, institutional leaders, and researchers need to clarify the purpose behind determining transfer rates. Is it to track students' use of the community college in pursuing a baccalaureate? If so, then including dual-credit and early admissions high school students seems appropriate, as does including any person who has enrolled at a community college and then transferred (as in the Oregon University System study). Or is the purpose to track only students who enter higher education through the community college (as in Grubb, 1991)? Alternatively, is the purpose to capture how the imprimatur of the community college curriculum affects students' subsequent performance in the four-year sector? In this case, the transfer student may be defined as one who has completed a particular degree program such as the A.A. or has earned enough credits (say, 50 or more) so that one could reasonably say there was a curricular effect of attending. In other words, is the purpose to capture student attendance patterns or measure the community college's institutional effectiveness in preparing students to achieve the baccalaureate?

In sum, a better job of tracking the various types of community college transfers must be done, whether at the institutional or the system level. Examining the transfer rates of different cohorts will provide a comparative perspective for policymakers and the general public and will also demonstrate the different ways students use the community college in their pursuit of the baccalaureate. Collecting this information will yield a more accurate picture of community college transfer rates. If that happens, cries of alarm about falling rates may even be recognized as false as Chicken Little's concerns about the sky.

References

Adelman, C. *Answers in the Tool Box: Academic Intensity, Attendance Patterns, and Bachelor's Degree Attainment.* Washington, D.C.: Office of Educational Research and Improvement, U.S. Department of Education, 1999.

Baldwin, A. "Indicators of the University Success of Associate Degree Recipients in the Fields of Business, Computer Science, and Engineering." *Journal of Applied Research in the Community College,* 1994, *1*, 113–128.

Banks, D. L. "Why a Consistent Definition of Transfer? An ERIC Review." *Community College Review,* 1990, *18*(2), 47–53.

Berkner, L., Horn, L., and Clune, M. *Descriptive Summary of 1995–96 Beginning Postsecondary Students: Three Years Later, with an Essay on Students Who Started at Less-Than-4-Year Institutions.* Washington, D.C.: National Center for Education Statistics, 2000.

Berman, P., Curry, J., Nelson, B., and Weiler, D. *Enhancing Transfer Effectiveness: A Model for the 1990s.* First Year Report to the National Effective Transfer Consortium, 1990. (ED 324 050)

Brawer, F. "Bad New/Good News: Collecting Transfer Data." *Community College Review,* 1991, *19*(3), 48–53.

Center for the Study of Community Colleges. *National Transfer Assembly Results: Update for 1995.* ERIC Clearinghouse for Community Colleges, EdInfo 01-04, 2001.

Clagett, C. A., and Huntington, R. B. "Assessing the Transfer Function: Data Exchanges and Transfer Rates." *Community College Review,* 1994, *22*(4), 21–26.

Cohen, A. M., and Brawer, F. B. *The American Community College.* (3rd ed.) San Francisco: Jossey-Bass, 1996.

Crooks, K. A. "State Sponsored College-Level Learning for High School Students: Selected Findings from a National Policy Study." *Learning Productivity News,* 1998, *4*(2), 10–12.

de los Santos, A. G., and Wright, I. "Maricopa's Swirling Students: Earning One-Third of Arizona State's Bachelor's Degrees," *AACJC Journal,* 1990, *60*(6), 32–34.

Dougherty, K. "Community Colleges and Baccalaureate Attainment." *Journal of Higher Education,* 1992, *63*(2), 188–214.

Dougherty, K. *The Contradictory College.* Albany: State University of New York Press, 1994.

Friedlander, J. "An ERIC Review: Why Is Transfer Education Declining?" *Community College Review,* 1980, *8*(2), 59–66.

Gelin, F. *Transfer Rates: How to Measure and for What Purpose?* Vancouver, Canada: British Columbia Council on Admission and Transfer, 1999.

Girardi, T., and Stein, R. "State Dual Credit Policy and Its Implications for Community Colleges: Lessons from Missouri for the 21st Century." B. K. Townsend and S. B. Twombly (eds.), *Educational Policy in the 21st Century,* Vol. 2: *Community Colleges: Policy in the Future Context.* Westport, Conn.: Ablex, 2001.

Grubb, N. "The Decline of Community College Transfer Rates: Evidence from National Longitudinal Surveys." *Journal of Higher Education,* 1991, *62*(2), 194–222.

Lee, V. E., and Frank, K. A. "Students' Characteristics That Facilitate the Transfer from Two-Year to Four-Year Colleges." *Sociology of Education,* 1990, *63*, 178–193.

Nora, A. *Reexamining the Community College Mission.* New Expeditions Issues Paper no. 2. Washington, D.C.: Community College Press, 2000.

Nora, A., and Rendon, L. *Quantitative Outcomes of Student Progress.* New York: Ford Foundation, 1998.

Oregon University System, Office of Academic Affairs, and Oregon Department of Community Colleges and Workforce Development. *Students Who Transfer Between Oregon Community Colleges and Oregon University System Institutions: What the Data Say.* Salem: Oregon University System, Office of Academic Affairs, and Oregon Department of Community Colleges and Workforce Development, 2000.

Palmer, J. C. "The Characteristics and Education Objectives of Students Served by Community College Vocational Curricula." *DAI,* 1987, *48*, 2794A. University Microfilms no. DA8800613.

Porter, S. R. "Including Transfer-Out Behavior in Retention Models: Using the NSLC Enrollment Search Data." Paper presented at the North East Association of Institutional Research Conference, Newport, R.I., 1999.

Tinto, V. "Colleges and Communities: Taking Research on Student Persistence Seriously." *Review of Higher Education,* 1998, *21*(2), 167–178.

BARBARA K. TOWNSEND *is professor of higher education and associate dean for research and development in the College of Education, University of Missouri-Columbia. She is also a former community college faculty member and administrator.*

3

Drawing on recent research, this chapter provides insights into contemporary postsecondary vocational models and delivery strategies. The strengths and weaknesses of various vocational models are discussed, including what research says about program effectiveness and student outcomes.

Contemporary Vocational Models and Programs: What the Research Tells Us

Debra D. Bragg

Throughout the twentieth century and into the twenty-first, two-year colleges have strengthened their commitment to vocational education. Programs to prepare students for immediate employment in occupational and technical fields continue alongside newer models emphasizing a wide range of employment and further educational opportunities. New models emerged in the 1990s, often with federal and state support, emphasizing workforce preparation and workforce development for both traditional and nontraditional students. Frequently, these models and related programs attempt to strengthen for-credit and non-credit-generating options on behalf of enhanced workforce and economic development. The new vocational models and programs are aimed at attracting students who seek the bachelor's degree, including traditional-age students who enter directly from high school in technical preparation (tech prep) and school-to-work transition programs, with the intention of preparing more high school students to transition into college after completing rigorous academics and career-technical education at the secondary level.

The new vocational programs are also attracting a growing population of reverse transfer students who choose technical careers in community colleges after attending a four-year college. Reverse transfer students include individuals who participated in a baccalaureate degree program and then returned to the community college for associate degree education. They also include bachelor's or higher graduates who are attending a community college for the first time after completing their degree because they are seeking skills in high-tech occupations. Increasingly, short-term certificates are offered by community colleges for Workforce Investment Act (WIA) clients, and these students often come to college to prepare for external, vendor-specific certification examinations such as those for Microsoft or Novell Engineer.

Striving to overcome image problems of the past, some vocational programs are referred to as the "shadow college" (Jacobs and Teahen, 1997) because they are so new or so transformed from prior vocational offerings that they are not classified as vocational in the traditional sense of providing preparation for immediate employment through terminal education programs. Research suggests that significant reforms of vocational education have begun, though the effectiveness of these efforts is sometimes less than certain. Vocational models and programs supported with legislation such as the federal Carl D. Perkins Vocational and Technical Education Act (referred to as Perkins III) and WIA are the most likely to be scrutinized with formal research and evaluation, but even these initiatives are so new that conclusive results that might be useful in improving practice are still in short supply.

The Changing Vocational Education Enterprise

Today's two-year colleges, particularly community colleges, have a major responsibility for preparing the nation's current and future mid-skilled workforce, a workforce that accounts for three-fourths of all employees in America (Carnevale, 2000; Carnevale and Desrochers, 2001; Grubb, 1996). To address the needs of this segment of the labor force, community colleges continue to deliver programs that have existed for many years, such as business, nursing, industrial, and manufacturing technologies; agriculture; and early childhood education. Added to these older ones are programs in such "hot" fields as information technologies, biotechnology, telecommunications, and nuclear medicine technology (Phillippe and Valiga, 2000). Increasingly, these new programs use the tech prep model, which links secondary and postsecondary education to ensure that students' academic education in high school prepares them for the postsecondary level (Bragg, 2001a). These programs are not geared, however, for older students who are already employed and seeking new skills through short-term training and marketable credentials.

With public two-year colleges enrolling well over five million full-time-equivalent students nationwide (National Center for Education Statistics, 1999a, 1999b), an estimated 2.5 million students are enrolled in public postsecondary vocational education each year. Based on the 1995–96 National Postsecondary Student Aid Study, Levesque and colleagues (2000) reported that one-half of the students who engage in public for-credit collegiate studies below the bachelor's level major in a vocational field. Of the remaining group, about 23 percent enroll in an academic field, and another 28 percent do not report a major, which suggests that the actual enrollment in vocational education could be higher.

Setting out a terminology that is useful in comprehending the shifts occurring in postsecondary vocational education and paralleling an earlier typology created by Kantor (1997), Warford and Flynn (2000) categorize students served by vocational programs in four worker groups. Warford and Flynn describe the first group of students as *emerging* workers or workforce learners, a group of students who are traditional college age (twenty-two years or younger) and preparing for entry-level employment. Secondary-to-postsecondary programs such as tech prep and school-to-work transition are emphasized for these students. The second group is the *transitional* workers or learners, who are accessing vocational programs to help them move from one job or career to another or from unemployment into the workforce. Vocational programs serving displaced workers and persons receiving public assistance fit into this group, as do recipients of WIA Individual Training Accounts.

The third category is composed of *entrepreneurial* workers or learners. These individuals seek assistance from two-year colleges to assist them in starting or operating small to medium-sized businesses, often using the college to train their employees through weekend courses and noncredit seminars. *Incumbent* workers or learners make up the fourth category. They seek vocational programs focused on upgrading current job skills, often through accelerated training that may or may not provide college credit. Warford and Flynn (2000) argue that this typology is beneficial because it moves two-year college educators beyond a preoccupation with the conventional vocational program emphasizing full-time study for entry-level employment.

Recognizing differences by institutional type and mission, approximately half of full-time faculty are engaged in some teaching of vocational subjects on two-year college campuses. Usually, an even larger percentage of part-time faculty are engaged in vocational teaching, and these individuals are typically drawn from the local workforce (Palmer and Zimbler, 2000). Confirming the community orientation of vocational programs, Brewer and Gray (1997) concluded that vocational faculty are more acutely aware of and engaged in community issues than their academic counterparts. Whereas academic faculty saw little need to link with their communities and therefore devoted minimal time to these activities, vocational faculty, particularly those who are full-time, assume responsibility for forging partnerships to build program enrollments and address community needs. As the need for highly trained employees increases, vocational faculty are likely to experience more pressure to develop partnerships with firms in their communities.

Research on Vocational Curricula and Programs

To understand better the impact of vocational education, it is necessary to examine the research results associated with various programs, models, and strategies, including implementation issues, and available evidence on program effectiveness and outcomes associated with student participation.

Traditional Occupational and Technical Programs. Two-year colleges engaging in vocational education often refer to their long-standing programs as occupational, technical, or career programs. Usually, these programs provide students with certification or licensure in a particular career field, and many of these programs culminate in an associate degree, often an associate of applied science (A.A.S.) degree (though the type of associate degree awarded varies somewhat by state). Programs in business, health care, engineering, and related technologies; computer and information technologies; and child care enroll the preponderance of today's students in postsecondary vocational education (Boesel and McFarland, 1994; Cohen and Brawer, 1996).

In one of the most comprehensive studies of the U.S. vocational system, including postsecondary vocational education, the National Assessment of Vocational Education, in what is referred to as the NAVE study (Boesel and McFarland, 1994), concluded that postsecondary vocational enrollments are stable or growing at about the same pace as general enrollments. Examining efforts of postsecondary vocational programs to respond to federal legislation passed during the 1990s emphasizing academic and vocational integration, the NAVE study reported positive results for postsecondary vocational education but also recognized some concerns. Specifically, the study concluded that postsecondary vocational programs have not adopted integrated academic and vocational curricula as readily as the secondary level, and academic and vocational integration is a required component of federal vocational legislation of the 1990s. More recent research has supported this conclusion, with studies by Grubb, Badway, Bell, and Kraskouskas (1996) and Perin (2000) reporting movement on curriculum integration but significant roadblocks as well. In a study of academic and vocational integration in Illinois community colleges, Bragg and Reger (2000) concluded that the majority of community colleges were offering stand-alone applied academics courses, but more sophisticated integration models, such as paired courses and learning communities, were much less evident.

Looking at the demographic characteristics of students in vocational programs, Levesque and her colleagues (2000) have confirmed historic enrollment patterns that suggest the likelihood of majoring in a vocational field increases as family income declines, emphasizing the importance of financial aid to support postsecondary vocational participation. In terms of enrollment by racial or ethnic groups, extant results are contradictory, undoubtedly due to the complex effects of socioeconomic status. For instance, Levesque and colleagues indicate that vocational enrollment declines in public subbaccalaureate programs if students are African American (this result is not evident for other racial or ethnic groups), whereas results of the NAVE study by Boesel, Hudson, Deich, and Masten (1994) show African Americans overrepresented in postsecondary vocational education, mirroring secondary vocational education. Moreover, postsecondary vocational programs are more likely than other subbaccalaureate programs to enroll students who are economically or educationally disadvantaged, are disabled, or are single parents.

Tech Prep and School-to-Work Transition Programs. The federal Carl D. Perkins legislation of 1990 authorized planning and implementation of technical education (tech prep). Charged with supporting a multitude of goals and learner needs, tech prep programs are intended to establish formal articulation agreements by identifying a logical progression of integrated and rigorous academic and vocational courses from the secondary to the postsecondary level, leading to the A.A.S. degree. Through at least a two-plus-two sequential curriculum (or additional years of education before or after the two-plus-two), tech prep can prepare for college students who might not otherwise pursue careers requiring postsecondary-level math, science, and technological studies. National studies of tech prep implementation by Boesel, Rahn, and Deich (1994); Bragg and colleagues (1999; see also Bragg, 2001b); and Hershey, Silverberg, Owens, and Hulsey (1998) show advancement in tech prep implementation over the decade of the 1990s, with the vast majority of U.S. school districts and nearly all two-year colleges participating. These studies also show enhancements in partnerships between secondary schools, community colleges, businesses, and community organizations; and within these organizations, more collaboration has occurred among academic and vocational instructors because of professional development and curriculum alignment efforts.

Even though implementation has progressed, little is known about how tech prep participants have transitioned from the secondary to the postsecondary level, nor are all of the potential benefits of transition programs evident. Undoubtedly, it is difficult to assess student outcomes before an educational program is fully implemented, so the evolving nature of tech prep has slowed research on student outcomes. Addressing this dilemma, a four-year longitudinal study (Bragg and others, 1999) that is nearing completion is showing that the majority of high school tech prep participants transition to two-year colleges, although their transition may not be simple or direct. Some attend only four-year colleges, but many move back and forth between the two- and four-year systems. Nearly all work while attending college as well. Since schools consider many tech prep students "non-college-bound," these results are important because they suggest that tech prep may be a viable launching pad for higher education for high school students. However, factors that put any college student at risk, such as competing priorities with work and family, need to be given careful consideration.

School-to-Work and Work-Based Learning Programs. In addition to tech prep, other legislation has had a facilitative effect on recent vocational program reforms, specifically the School-to-Work Opportunities Act of 1994, commonly referred to as STWOA. Key goals of STWOA include secondary-to-postsecondary articulation to enhance transition to college, business partnerships to enhance curriculum development, work-based learning opportunities, and systemic changes in coordination to enhance educational and economic benefits for all students. Career academies are another new model linked closely with school-to-work, and these academies have proliferated throughout the country, with evaluation results suggesting a positive impact on students' transition to college at either the two-year or four-year level (see, for example, Maxwell and Rubin, 1997).

Work-based learning (WBL) was revitalized at the postsecondary level during the 1990s as well, although research suggests that these efforts were targeted more toward career preparation than toward exploration, as is often the case at the secondary level. Still, nearly one out of five students in postsecondary vocational programs are estimated to participate in WBL in a wide range of occupational fields (Bragg, Hamm, and Trinkle, 1995; Bragg and Hamm, 1996). Although WBL is seldom required, because of the long-standing commitment to WBL by the health professions, virtually all community colleges offer health-related WBL opportunities, typically using intensive professional and clinical models. Challenges to offering more WBL in the immediate future include the high cost of these programs, difficulties in coordinating WBL for adult students who already hold jobs, and waning commitment by employers over the long term, except for students demonstrating the most potential for employment. Questions about the viability of WBL in the long term are even more serious due to the impending expiration of the STWOA legislation.

Transfer and Applied Baccalaureate Programs. Today, traditional vocational programs are shedding their dead-end image by encouraging the transfer option (Townsend, 1999). No doubt difficulties exist in transferring credits for students completing vocational programs, since credits associated with vocational courses often do not transfer. However, national studies (see, for example, Cohen and Ignash, 1994; Praeger, 1988) suggest that more vocational students are choosing to enroll in two-year vocational programs and then transfer to four-year colleges (especially regional public universities, small private colleges, and proprietary colleges offering bachelor's degrees), which are also increasingly vocationally oriented. Transfer into these applied baccalaureate degree programs is facilitated to ensure that more community college students gain the opportunity to matriculate at senior institutions through the acceptance of technical course credits earned at the two-year college. Although this is a truly powerful idea, efforts to establish sequential curricula to assist more learners in moving from secondary to two-year to four-year institutions meet with strong resistance. Misalignment in curricular content and academic standards is evident at all levels, and these gaps and inefficiencies are not entirely haphazard (Orr and Bragg, 2001), since education has historically been relied on for the selection and placement of students in different levels of employment. Consequently, few applied baccalaureate degree programs exist in four-year colleges (such as the one at Southern Illinois University) or on the state level (as in Maryland), but interest in establishing these programs is growing nationwide.

Townsend (2001) reports that nationally, students with the A.A.S. degree are transferring in numbers equal to or greater than students with the traditional transfer degrees (Cohen and Ignash, 1994). In fact, there is evidence that many students in vocational programs intend to transfer to a four-year college or university at the time they enter the two-year schools. Unfortunately, little research has followed vocational program participants or A.A.S. recipients into four-year programs, thus restricting our knowledge about the transfer experience for these students.

Workforce Training Programs: For-Credit and Noncredit. Sometimes linked to traditional vocational curricula but increasingly tied to continuing education and community service divisions, two-year colleges are engaging in a host of education-business partnership arrangements, characterized by Grubb and others (1997, p. ix) as "entrepreneurial" colleges. Indeed, firm-specific contractual or customized training has become increasingly important and is thought to account for a growing percentage of two-year college enrollments (although exact figures are not available). These programs can be offered for credit or not for credit, depending on the needs of the firm and the desire of the individual students. These entrepreneurial initiatives are growing because they enhance college revenues, bring greater visibility to the colleges in the community and the region, and meet learner needs for certification and immediate employment.

In addition to customized training, offerings in a wide range of general workforce and career and technical areas are proliferating, some offered for credit but many on a noncredit basis. Phillippe and Valiga (2000) confirm in *Faces of the Future* that noncredit enrollment is rising. They portray noncredit students as even more diverse than credit-seeking students, representing a broader range of ages, more likely to have a bachelor's degree, and more likely of low-income status and seeking immediate employment. Phillippe and Valiga note that the high level of diversity among noncredit students reflects the numerous noncredit options offered by community colleges, including contracted training with business and industry, computer training, personal enrichment courses, and ESL and GED courses. These new certification programs offer some of the greatest challenges but also some of the most intriguing opportunities as community colleges consider how to deliver vocational education and workforce development options in the future.

Conclusion

As two-year colleges move forward, it is important to examine the postsecondary vocational enterprise, to raise questions about the changing nature of vocational education, and to review what research can tell us about ways to improve programs. Through the lenses of carefully applied research, combined with the valuable experiences of community college practitioners, we can gain a better understanding of vocational education and the prominent role that it plays in the educational system. The student populations will continue to evolve, and vocational programs must therefore work more aggressively to meet diverse learners' needs. New programs such as tech prep that encourage learners to transition from high school to college, new delivery systems that encourage enrollment by transitional learners, and new models that serve students via short-term training (for credit or not) are welcome additions to the community college curriculum. These programs need visionary leadership to be successful, and they need the support of creative partnerships between the state and local levels and between business, community, and other educational partners in the local context.

There are healthy signs from research on vocational programs that policies and practices are changing. Even though federal legislation continues to emphasize secondary vocational education, there are indications that postsecondary vocational education is gaining in importance. Funding for postsecondary vocational programs is rising, and new models such as tech prep emphasize the importance of secondary-to-postsecondary articulation and seamless curricula, encouraging smoother transition to college. Even so, these programs make up only a small portion of the total enrollment of postsecondary vocational education, which increasingly serves adult learners in alternative delivery modes in both for-credit and noncredit formats. Very little is currently known about these proliferating program options or the students who participate in them. The outcomes of these programs are also unclear, making it difficult to extrapolate lessons for program improvement.

Indeed, evidence of program effectiveness as indicated through student outcomes is difficult to pinpoint for vocational education, though admittedly outcomes assessment associated with vocational education may well have advanced farther than other parts of the curriculum. Still, much remains to be done to evaluate outcomes associated with vocational education that can inform faculty about how to design curricula and develop learner-centered instruction. Moving beyond the standard kinds of retention, completion, and placement outcomes that have dominated federally funded accountability systems may be difficult, but it must be done, for the benefit of the students. Educators and employers have a clear stake in reformed vocational programs, and they need to be informed about how the new programs are working. Without question, more effective decisions can be made when such information is available.

References

Boesel, D., Hudson, L., Deich, S., and Masten, C. *National Assessment of Vocational Education: Final Report to Congress, Vol. 2: Participation in and Quality of Vocational Education.* Washington, D.C.: Office of Educational Research and Improvement, U.S. Department of Education, 1994.

Boesel, D., and McFarland, L. *National Assessment of Vocational Education: Final Report to Congress, Vol. 1: Summary and Recommendations.* Washington, D.C.: Office of Educational Research and Improvement, U.S. Department of Education, 1994.

Boesel, D., Rahn, M., and Deich, S. *National Assessment of Vocational Education, Final Report to Congress*, Vol. 3: *Program Improvement: Educational Reform*. Washington, D.C.: Office of Educational Research and Improvement, U.S. Department of Education, 1994.

Bragg, D. D. "Opportunities and Challenges for the New Vocationalism in American Community Colleges." In D. D. Bragg (ed.), *The New Vocationalism in American Community Colleges*. New Directions for Community Colleges, no. 115. San Francisco: Jossey-Bass, 2001a.

Bragg, D. D. *Promising Outcomes for Eight Local Tech Prep Consortia: A Summary of Initial Results*. Saint Paul: National Research Center for Career and Technical Education, University of Minnesota, 2001b.

Bragg, D., and Hamm, R. *Linking College and Work: Exemplary Policies and Practices of Two-Year College Work-Based Learning Programs*. Berkeley: National Center for Research in Vocational Education, University of California, 1996. (MDS-721)

Bragg, D. D., Hamm, R. E., and Trinkle, K. A. *Work-Based Learning in Two-Year Colleges in the United States*. Berkeley: National Center for Research in Vocational Education, University of California, 1995. (MDS-795)

Bragg, D. D., and Reger, W. "Toward a More Unified Education: Academic and Vocational Integration in Illinois Community Colleges." *Journal of Vocational Education Research*, 2000, 25(3), 237–272.

Bragg, D. D., and others. *Tech Prep Implementation and Preliminary Outcomes for Eight Local Tech Prep Consortia*. Berkeley: National Center for Research in Vocational Education, University of California, 1999. (MDS-1314)

Brewer, D., and Gray, M. "Connecting College and Community in the New Economy? An Analysis of Community College Faculty-Labor Market Linkages." Berkeley: National Center for Research in Vocational Education, University of California, 1997. (RAND/RP-663)

Carnevale, A. P. *Community Colleges and Career Qualifications*. Issues Paper no. 11. Washington, D.C.: Community College Press, 2000.

Carnevale, A. P., and Desrochers, D. *Help Wanted . . . Credentials Required: Community Colleges in the Knowledge Economy*. Princeton, N.J.: Educational Testing Service, 2001.

Cohen, A. M., and Brawer, F. B. *The American Community College*. (3rd ed.) San Francisco: Jossey-Bass, 1996.

Cohen, A., and Ignash, J. M. "An Overview of the Total Credit Curriculum." In A. M. Cohen (ed.), *Relating Curriculum and Transfer*. New Directions for Community Colleges, no. 86. San Francisco: Jossey-Bass, 1994.

Grubb, W. N. *Working in the Middle: Strengthening Education and Training for the Mid-Skilled Labor Force*. San Francisco: Jossey-Bass, 1996.

Grubb, W. N., Badway, N., Bell, D., and Kraskouskas, E. *Community College Innovations in Workforce Preparation: Curriculum Integration and Tech Prep*. Mission Viejo, CA: League for Innovation in the Community College, National Center for Research in Vocational Education, and National Council for Occupational Education, 1996.

Grubb, W. N., and others. *Workforce, Economic, and Community Development: The Changing Landscape of the Entrepreneurial Community College*. Mission Viejo, Calif.: League for Innovation in the Community College, 1997.

Hershey, A. M., Silverberg, M. K., Owens, T., and Hulsey, L. K. *Focus for the Future: The Final Report of the National Tech Prep Evaluation*. Princeton, N.J.: Mathematica Policy Research, 1998.

Jacobs, J., and Teahen, R. *The Shadow College and NCA Accreditation: A Conceptual Framework*. Macomb, Mich.: Macomb Community College, 1997.

Kantor, S. "Rethinking the Role of Instruction for Workforce Training." In T. Zeiss (ed.), *Developing the World's Best Workforce*. Washington, D.C.: Community College Press, 1997.

Levesque, K., and others. *Vocational Education in the United States: Toward the Year 2000*. Washington, D.C.: Office of Educational Research and Improvement, U.S. Department of Education, 2000.

Maxwell, N. L., and Rubin, V. *The Relative Impact of a Career Academy on Postsecondary Work and Education Skills in Urban Public High Schools.* Hayward: Human Investment Research and Education Center, California State University, 1997.
National Center for Education Statistics. *Integrated Postsecondary Education Data System (IPEDS) Fall Enrollment Survey.* Washington, D.C.: U.S. Department of Education, 1999a.
National Center for Education Statistics. *Integrated Postsecondary Education Data System (IPEDS) Institutional Characteristics Survey.* Washington, D.C.: U.S. Department of Education, 1999b.
Orr, M. T., and Bragg, D. D. "Policy Directions for K–14 Education: Looking to the Future." In B. K. Townsend and S. B. Twombly (eds.), *Educational Policy in the 21st Century,* Vol. 2: *Community Colleges: Policy in the Future Context.* Westport, Conn.: Ablex, 2001.
Palmer, J., and Zimbler, L. *Instructional Faculty and Staff in Public 2-Year Colleges.* Washington, D.C.: Office of Educational Research and Improvement, U.S. Department of Education, 2000.
Perin, D. "Curriculum and Pedagogy to Integrate Occupational and Academic Instruction in the Community College: Implications for Faculty Development." *CCRC Brief,* Mar. 2000, pp. 1–4.
Phillippe, K. A., and Valiga, M. J. *Faces of the Future: A Portrait of American Community College Students.* Washington, D.C.: Community College Press, 2000.
Praeger, C. "The Other Transfer Degree." In C. Prager (ed.), *Enhancing Articulation and Transfer.* New Directions for Community Colleges, no. 61. San Francisco: Jossey-Bass, 1988.
Townsend, B. K. "Reassessing the Transfer Function." Paper presented at the annual meeting of the Association for the Study of Higher Education, San Antonio, Tex., Nov. 1999.
Townsend, B. K. "Blurring the Lines: Transforming Terminal Education to Transfer Education." In D. D. Bragg (ed.), *The New Vocationalism in American Community Colleges.* New Directions for Community Colleges, no. 115. San Francisco: Jossey-Bass, 2001.
Warford, L., and Flynn, W. J. "New Game, New Rules: The Workforce Development Challenge." *Leadership Abstracts,* 2000, 13(2), 1–4.

DEBRA D. BRAGG *is an associate professor and director of the Office of Community College Research and Leadership at the University of Illinois at Urbana-Champaign. She is also the university's site director for the National Centers for Career and Technical Education.*

*One of the community college's important functions is to
provide remedial instruction for traditional-age and adult
students who are not prepared for college-level work.
This chapter explores areas of agreement and
disagreement in policy and practice. Given the challenges
presented by a large and diverse underprepared
population, there is no "one size fits all" solution.*

Remediation at the Community College: Pressing Issues, Uncertain Solutions

Betsy Oudenhoven

Remediation in higher education is a complicated issue that has complex causes, uncertain solutions, and critical implications for both education and society. This chapter concentrates on community college students and programs and explores areas of agreement and disagreement in research, policy, and practice. The focus is on underprepared students who are native speakers of English and on the functions of assessment, placement, and coursework in addressing and remediating their academic deficiencies. Although remedial coursework is only one part of a developmental approach that could also include tutoring, academic support services, advising, and counseling, it appears to be the most controversial part of the developmental education equation. While community college educators agree that remediation is an important function, there is disagreement, or at least lack of consensus, over how students should be assessed, placed, and taught.

The Buck Stops Where? A Higher Education and Public Policy Debate

Despite the fact that higher education has a long history of serving underprepared students, the issue of remediation is currently at the center of a number of heated educational and social debates. How or even whether higher education should address the needs of students who are not prepared for college-level work is a divisive issue, reflective of enduring debates over access and educational standards.

Opponents of college remediation argue that the availability of remediation in college removes incentives to do well in high school, detracts from the education of prepared college students by "dumbing down" courses, and leads to low graduation rates. Some taxpayers and state boards of education insist that colleges should not teach what high schools have already received tax dollars to provide. Many four-year institutions maintain that remedial courses are not college-level and are therefore not their responsibility; some colleges are concerned over the perceived loss of institutional prestige or status if they enroll remedial students; and other institutions argue that resources allocated to remedial education should more appropriately be directed to degree programs (Astin, 1999; Breneman and Haarlow, 1998; Phipps, 1998; Roueche and Roueche, 1999).

Those who advocate offering remediation at all levels of higher education argue that shifting full responsibility for remediation to the two-year schools may be unfair to both the colleges and the students. They suggest that isolating remedial education in the community colleges creates a "caste system" between two-year and four-year institutions and may limit opportunities for students (Astin, 1999; Boylan, 1995; Brint and Karabel, 1995; Schrag, 1999). The increased numbers of underprepared students could tax community college resources to the breaking point. Boylan (1995) also cautions that some four-year institutions may not be able to afford the loss of enrollment that would ensue. In addition, states could experience an exodus from public education to private education or even to out-of-state institutions as students seek out colleges that will welcome them and offer the courses and services they need.

The recent high-profile controversy over remediation in the City University of New York (CUNY) system catapulted the issue over who should be responsible for underprepared students into the consciousness of both the public and higher education professionals (Schrag, 1999). In 1970, the CUNY system adopted an open admissions policy that virtually assured every New York City high school graduate a place in the system. For many proponents of open admissions, this symbolized CUNY's commitment to immigrants, minorities, and the poor. Twenty-five years later, high remediation rates and low graduation rates led to criticism and political pressure, eventually resulting in a May 1998 decision by the CUNY board of trustees to phase out remediation at CUNY's four-year colleges and limit community college remediation to one year.

Since the CUNY decision, several significant studies of remediation have been conducted (Breneman and Haarlow, 1998; McCabe, 2000; McCabe and Day, 1998; Phipps, 1998; Roueche and Roueche, 1999). As a result of this increased study and scrutiny, many educators and researchers have reached the conclusion that remediation is one of the most important and most pressing educational, social, and economic issues in the United States today (Astin, 1999; McCabe and Day, 1998; Schrag, 1999). Remediation, these researchers argue, is not the problem; it is the solution to meeting the educational needs of large numbers of students who might otherwise never become productive members of a society that desperately needs their contributions.

Although much of the current debate over remediation focuses on where it should occur, there is almost universal consensus among community colleges that serving underprepared students is an important part of the community college mission. Open-door admissions policies, affordable tuition, convenient locations, an emphasis on teaching and learning, and a welcoming attitude make community colleges a logical starting place for many of these students. The often cited National Center for Education Statistics (NCES) report, *Remedial Education at Higher Education Institutions in Fall 1995* (1996), indicated that 100 percent of community colleges offered remediation and 41 percent of community college freshmen enrolled in at least one precollegiate course. McCabe and Day (1998) estimate that approximately half of all students entering community colleges need some form of remediation.

Assessing Students: Lack of Consistent Standards and Policies

Most community colleges assess incoming students in reading, writing, and math, and most institutions are very clear about the criteria they use to do this. However, there is not complete consensus among institutions on what constitutes "college-level" work. For example, some institutions do not consider college algebra a transferable college-level math course, while others do; consequently, there is not complete agreement about who needs remediation (Merisotis and Phipps, 2000; Phipps, 1998). Astin (1998, p. 13) notes that "most remedial students turn out to be simply those who have the lowest scores on some sort of normative measurement—standardized tests, school grades and the like. But where we draw the line is completely arbitrary: lowest quarter, lowest fifth, lowest 5 percent, or what? Nobody knows." Although individual institutions may have definitive standards for identifying remedial students, "the line" is not consistent throughout higher education.

Measuring and defining remedial students occurs primarily at the institutional level. Community colleges do not necessarily require ACT or SAT scores, more often relying on high school grades, GED scores, TOEFL scores, and the results of their own assessment instruments. Individual institutions determine which of their students they will assess and what instruments and measures they will use, with no national and minimal state consistency. As a result, there is little agreement on who is a remedial student.

The inconsistency in definition and procedures is potentially problematic for transfer students who must take different assessment tests and meet different standards from institution to institution. Most colleges grant institutional credit for remedial courses, but this credit does not transfer. This loss of credit and time is extremely frustrating to students, many of whom are confused by why standards met at one postsecondary institution are not considered sufficient at another.

Whereas most institutions assess students in basic skills areas, policies and procedures for assessment differ, including when assessments are conducted during students' course of study. In addition, given the diversity of the community college population, it may not be necessary to assess all students (for example, returning adult students enrolled in one or two courses to improve workplace skills should probably be exempted). Because community colleges are committed to serving all students, one of their greatest challenges is determining which policies, programs, and pedagogical approaches will lead students to success in achieving their varied and individual goals. The balancing act is to enact interventions that will provide help where needed, without penalizing (or frustrating) students for whom the policy is not intended.

Who Needs Remediation? A Large and Diverse Population

There is little dispute that many high school graduates need additional assistance in the basic skills areas of reading, writing, and math. Although the percentage of remedial students has not increased in the past twenty or thirty years, the sheer number of students seeking postsecondary education has increased, including a dramatic growth in nonnative speakers of English (Adelman, 1996). Adelman found no significant percentage increase in the number of students taking remedial courses between 1973 and 1982 (48 percent) and between 1983 and 1992 (46 percent), a result borne out by NCES surveys in 1983, 1989, and 1995 (Breneman and Haarlow, 1999). However, between 1989 and 1995, the number of students enrolled in higher education increased by half a million (Phipps, 1998). McCabe (2000) cites statistics indicating that annually more than one million students enroll in remedial courses (20 percent of them in reading, 25 percent in writing, and 34 percent in math).

These students are often lumped as a group in categories such as "underprepared," "remedial," or "developmental," but as the diversity of students seeking postsecondary education has increased, so has the diversity of the population needing remedial assistance. Underprepared students are "bipolar" in terms of age as well as the length of time that they have been away from education (Ignash, 1997). They are traditional-age students attending immediately after high school; adult students who have served in the military, worked, or raised families; and students for whom English is not their first language. Their educational, cultural, and socioeconomic backgrounds differ, as do their motivations and goals for pursuing higher education. The extent of their need for remediation differs as well (Adelman, 1996; Ignash, 1997).

Much of the consternation over remedial education centers on traditional-age students. Critics both inside and outside education want to understand why 60 percent of the remedial population consists of students who attend college immediately after high school but are still not prepared for their "thirteenth year" (Ignash, 1997). Research shows that the most significant factor may be that remedial students did not participate in a college preparatory curriculum in high school, a factor highly correlated with readiness for college-level work (Boylan, 1999a; Merisotis and Phipps, 2000). However, a 1998 Maryland study found that even among students who completed a college preparatory curriculum, of those who went directly to a community college, 40 percent still needed math remediation, 20 percent needed English, and 25 percent needed reading (Merisotis and Phipps, 2000). Clearly, there is some incongruence between what colleges require and what high schools consider sufficient preparation in math and English.

Adult students, the other 40 percent of the remedial population, turn to higher education for a variety of reasons. Though not all require additional support, many do. Adult students decide to pursue postsecondary education to support new interests or career goals, to retool for employment purposes, or because they finally have the time and resources. Those who need remediation may be rusty, or like their eighteen-year-old classmates, they may never have learned the information the first time around. Critics of remediation are a little more supportive of older students who need some additional preparatory work, accepting the impact of time away from formal education as a legitimate reason for requiring additional help (Cronholm, 1999; Ignash, 1997). It is possible that some remedial students may also have undetected academic or physical problems. Unfortunately, many underprepared students have not had positive educational experiences and come to postsecondary education with high hopes but little confidence in their academic abilities (Jones and Watson, 1990; McCabe, 2000; Roueche and Roueche, 1999).

Students also vary in the areas of remediation needed and the extent of their need. The good news is that although many students require remediation, most do not need much. The 1996 NCES report found that at 95 percent of the institutions surveyed, the average student needed remediation for one year or less. Additional research has found that 80 percent of students need only one or two courses, and very few require four or more. Math is the most common area of remediation. Research has found that the prognosis for success is generally good for students who need only one or two remedial courses or remediation only in math (Adelman, 1996).

Research has also shown that students who need extensive remediation, assistance in multiple areas, or remediation in reading are less likely to be successful (Adelman, 1996; McCabe, 2000; Weissman, Bulakowski, and Jumisko, 1997). Adelman found that "the extent of a student's need for remediation is inversely related to his or her eventual completion of a degree" (1996, p. 2), and deficiencies in reading significantly lower a student's chances of completing a degree. Weissman, Bulakowski, and Jumisko

(1997) also conclude that multiple deficiencies, reading deficiencies, and minority status place students at high risk for failure.

Given the odds for students who need extensive remediation, is it worth the effort? Research indicates that it is. In a study of college transcripts from the high school class of 1982, Adelman (1998) found that 60 percent of students who did not need any remediation earned a degree, compared to 35 percent of those who required five or more remedial classes. Despite the fact that degree completion rates fell as the need for remediation increased, Adelman's analysis showed that over one-third of the academically weakest students did eventually earn a degree. Boylan (1999b) asserts that with the appropriate interventions, underprepared students can be as successful in higher education as their college-ready counterparts. The National Study of College Remediation supports this assertion. The study found that of 1,520 community college students who began their remediation in 1990, nearly half completed their programs successfully, and the successfully remediated students went on to perform well in standard college work (McCabe, 2000). The study also found that a significantly lower percentage of seriously deficient students were successful and suggested that these students may require unique approaches to goal-setting and program delivery.

Placement in Remedial Courses: Rejecting the "Right to Fail"

Colleges continue to struggle with which policies and practices are both most efficient and most effective. One of the recommendations in the American Association of Community Colleges' publication *The Knowledge Net* is that community colleges "must make remedial courses mandatory for all learners who need them" (2000, p. 19). In a review of the community college literature, Weissman, Bulakowski, and Jumisko (1997) conclude that mandatory placement is related to academic success and argue that it should occur in the first year or even upon initial enrollment at the community college. They suggest that multiple deficiencies need to be addressed before other college-level work is permitted, although students requiring less remediation could simultaneously enroll in regular classes. This makes sense for native English speakers who may need remediation in math but are prepared in reading and writing or for those who need additional help with writing but can simultaneously take math, science, or other introductory general education courses that do not require extensive writing. The same may not be true for students of English as a second language, who may be strong in math or science but may have difficulty reading, speaking, and writing in classes where the instruction and the textbooks are in English.

The National Association for Developmental Education (NADE) also passed a resolution in March 1998 supporting "institutional policies that require mandatory academic assessment of incoming students and mandatory placement of students into developmental courses or services as appropriate." NADE cites NCES statistics indicating that 60 percent of institutions offered entry-level testing of all entering students, 75 percent required students to enroll in developmental courses based on this testing, and 66 percent placed some restrictions on regular coursework while students were enrolled in developmental courses. The NADE publication also cited results from a National Center for Developmental Education (NCDE) study of six thousand students that showed that mandatory testing and placement increased the likelihood of students' successfully completing their developmental courses.

Providing Instruction in Basic Skills: Isolation or Integration?

A controversial issue in the delivery of remedial courses is whether basic skills should be offered separately or embedded in the regular college curriculum (Boylan, 1999a, 1999b; "From Remediation," 1999; Jones and Watson, 1990; McCusker, 1999; McGrath and Townsend, 1997). Institutional and curricular responses to this issue vary. Some institutions require separate basic skills coursework, usually in reading or writing (or both), to precede any other college-level work. Students needing developmental work in math are almost always required to complete it prior to enrolling in a higher-level math class. However, some community colleges are experimenting with either embedding critical thinking and basic skills work in regular college classes or allowing students to simultaneously complete remedial and college-level work (Boylan, 1999a; "From Remediation," 1999; McCabe and Day, 1998; McCusker, 1999; Roueche and Roueche, 1999). The correlation between the perceived usefulness of a subject and academic achievement might argue for embedding remedial skill building into the standard college curriculum so that students are receiving attention to reading and writing in a context that has meaning for them. Proponents of this approach argue that it is sounder in terms of learning theory and prevents students from becoming discouraged at the additional time and cost of taking separate remedial classes.

A more traditional approach assigns underprepared students to separate courses for remedial work in English or math (or both), sometimes taught through a developmental education department or division and sometimes housed in the English or math department. However, isolated basic skills courses have been found to be least likely to have a long-term effect on achievement and persistence (McCabe and Day, 1998; McCusker, 1999). Maxwell argues that stand-alone remedial courses negatively affect students' attitudes and expectations and "force students to take longer to finish degrees, lower their self-concepts, and make it more difficult for them to shed the image of being at-risk students" (1997, p. 8). In addition, many remedial classes are taught through rote and repetition as opposed to questioning and intellectual discourse ("From Remediation," 1999; Jones and Watson, 1990; McGrath and Spear, 1991). McCabe and Day (1998) suggest that students need to learn higher-order skills in analytical reasoning, critical thinking, and problem solving as well as the basics of reading, writing, and math.

Others argue that mixing prepared and underprepared students in the same classroom does a disservice to both and can lead to low morale for both students and teachers (Cronholm, 1999; Steinberg, 1998). Regular faculty are not trained to address literacy issues, as developmental specialists are; underprepared students might not get the assistance they need; and college-ready students may become frustrated at the pace of the class or the attention needed by their less-prepared classmates.

A number of promising alternatives to traditional course delivery are available, most of which have shown success with college-ready students and are being adapted for use with underprepared students as well. Boylan (1999a) provides a helpful summary of a number of these approaches, including supplemental instruction, learning communities and collaborative learning, paired or linked courses, first-year seminars, critical thinking instruction, and strategic learning. He suggests a systematic integration of these approaches with assessment and advising processes to provide more accessible alternatives to traditional remedial courses.

Conclusion

Community colleges welcome underprepared students as a critical part of their educational mission; however, agreeing to serve these students may be the only point of real consensus. There are no consistent standards for what constitutes a remedial student; assessment instruments and cutoff scores vary from institution to institution, even within the same state; placement in basic skills courses is not always required, despite assessed need; and although there are some promising alternatives to course delivery, basic skills are taught, more often than not, in traditional stand-alone classes with little connection to the regular curriculum. In addition, the underprepared population is large and diverse, students have a variety of goals, and many are resistant to taking remedial classes. Community college administrators are also justifiably concerned that increasing numbers of underprepared students may overwhelm limited resources and may adversely affect other important programs at these colleges.

Though there is little agreement on how to proceed, one important step is to better understand and communicate the different goals of community college students and to determine measures of success that take these goals into account. Many other questions also deserve additional attention: Why do some students succeed and others fail? What happens to the students who are not successful? What works best for different populations—adult students, traditional-age students, and students with serious deficiencies? What assessment instruments are most effective, and are there ways to standardize assessment, at least within states? What institutional policies most often contribute to student success? What methods of course delivery work best for different populations and different remedial needs? What kind of training and information do faculty and staff need to work most effectively with these students? Further exploration of these questions through the current literature and through future research may provide helpful insights for community college practitioners.

Underprepared learners have always been a part of higher education, and despite the challenges, they continue to seek opportunity at the door of academe. They know that higher education can provide a better life financially, as well as a richer and more informed life personally and intellectually. Community colleges are providing the opportunity, but much more needs to be done to effectively meet the challenges that these students present. Additional research, increased sharing of successful programs and approaches across institutions, and an ongoing dialogue about the challenges and rewards of serving underprepared students may help community college practitioners identify and reach consensus on the policies and practices that will most often lead to academic success.

References

Adelman, C. "The Truth About Remedial Work." *Chronicle of Higher Education,* Oct. 4, 1996, p. A56.

Adelman, C. "The Kiss of Death?: An Alternative View of College Remediation." *National CrossTalk,* Summer 1998 [http://www.highereducation.org/crosstalk/ct0798/voices0798-adelman.html].

American Association of Community Colleges. *The Knowledge Net.* Washington, D.C.: Community College Press, 2000.

Astin, A. W. "Higher Education and Civic Responsibility." Paper presented at the American Council on Education Conference on Civic Roles and Responsibilities, Washington, D.C., June 1998.

Astin, A. W. "Rethinking Academic 'Excellence.'" *Liberal Education,* 1999, *85*(2), 8–18.

Boylan, H. R. "Making the Case for Developmental Education." *Research in Developmental Education,* 1995, *12*(2), 1–4.

Boylan, H. R. "Exploring Alternatives to Remediation." *Journal of Developmental Education,* 1999a, *22*(3), 2–8.

Boylan, H. R. "Harvard Symposium 2000: Developmental Education: Demographics, Outcomes, and Activities." *Journal of Developmental Education,* 1999b, *23*(2), 2–8.

Breneman, D. W., and Haarlow, W. N. "Remedial Education: Costs and Consequences." July 1998 [http://www.edexcellence.net/library/remed.html].

Breneman, D. W., and Haarlow, W. N. "Establishing the Real Value of Remedial Education." *Chronicle of Higher Education,* Apr. 9, 1999, pp. B6–B7.

Brint, S., and Karabel, J. *The Diverted Dream: Community Colleges and the Promise of Educational Opportunity in America, 1900–1985.* New York: Oxford University Press, 1995.

Cronholm, L. "Why One College Jettisoned All Its Remedial Courses." *Chronicle of Higher Education,* Sept. 24, 1999 [http://chronicle.com/weekly/v46/i05/05b00601.htm].

"From Remediation to Acceleration: Raising the Bar in Developmental Education." *Change,* 1999, *31*(1), 57–60.

Ignash, J. M. "Who Should Provide Postsecondary Remedial/Developmental Education?" In J. M. Ignash (ed.), *Implementing Effective Policies for Remedial and Developmental Education.* New Directions for Community Colleges, no. 100. San Francisco: Jossey-Bass, 1997.

Jones, D. J., and Watson, B. C. *"High-Risk" Students in Higher Education: Future Trends.* ASHE-ERIC Higher Education Report no. 3. Washington, D.C.: School of Education and Human Development, George Washington University, 1990.

Maxwell, M. "What Are the Functions of a College Learning Assistance Center? 1997. (ED 413 031)

McCabe, R. H. *No One to Waste: A Report to Public Decision-Makers and Community College Leaders.* Washington, D.C.: Community College Press, 2000.

McCabe, R. H., and Day, P. R., Jr. (eds.). *Developmental Education: A Twenty-First-Century Social and Economic Imperative.* Mission Viejo, Calif.: League for Innovation in the Community College and The College Board, 1998.

McCusker, M. "ERIC Review: Effective Elements of Developmental Reading and Writing Programs." *Community College Review,* 1999, *27*(2), 93–105.

McGrath, D., and Spear, M. B. *The Academic Crisis of the Community College.* Albany: State University of New York Press, 1991.

McGrath, D., and Townsend, B. K. "Strengthening Preparedness of At-Risk Students." In J. G. Gaff, J. L. Ratcliff, and Associates, *Handbook of the Undergraduate Curriculum: A Comprehensive Guide to Purposes, Structures, Practices, and Change.* San Francisco: Jossey-Bass, 1997.

Merisotis, J. P., and Phipps, R. A. "Remedial Education in Colleges and Universities: What's Really Going On?" *Review of Higher Education,* 2000, *24*(1), 67–85.

National Association of Developmental Education. "Need for Mandatory Academic Testing and Placement of Students in Appropriate College Courses." Resolution approved Mar. 1, 1998, rev. July 31, 1998 [http://www.umkc.edu/cad/nade/nadedocs/pstspl98.html].

National Center for Education Statistics. *Remedial Education at Higher Education Institutions in Fall 1995.* Washington, D.C.: Office of Educational Research and Improvement, U.S. Department of Education, 1996.

Phipps, R. *College Remediation: What It Is, What It Costs, What's at Stake.* Washington, D.C.: Institute for Higher Education Policy, 1998.

Roueche, J. E., and Roueche, S. D. *High Stakes, High Performance: Making Remedial Education Work.* Washington, D.C.: Community College Press, 1999.

Schrag, P. "End of the Second Chance?" *American Prospect,* 1999 [http://web6.infotrac.galegroup.com].

Steinberg, L. "Commentaries." In D. W. Breneman and W. N. Haarlow, "Remedial Education: Costs and Consequences." July 1998 [http://www.edexcellence.net/library/remed.html].

Weissman, J., Bulakowski, C., and Jumisko, M. K. "Using Research to Evaluate Developmental Education Programs and Policies." In J. M. Ignash (ed.), *Implementing Effective Policies for Remedial and Developmental Education.* New Directions for Community Colleges, no. 100. San Francisco: Jossey-Bass, 1997.

BETSY OUDENHOVEN *is the director of counseling at the College of Lake County, Grayslake, Illinois, and a doctoral student at Loyola University, Chicago.*

This chapter explores five concerns central to community college English as a second language (ESL) programs: the diversity within the community college ESL population, the place of ESL within the institution, employment and training issues for ESL instructors, "Generation 1.5," and financial and funding concerns.

English as a Second Language at the Community College: An Exploration of Context and Concerns

Amy J. Blumenthal

Community colleges have been instrumental in providing instruction in English as a second language (ESL), and statistics indicate that there is substantial need for such instruction. In 1991, some 40 percent of community colleges offered ESL instruction, but this percentage jumped to 55 percent by 1999 (Schuyler, 1999). Fitzgerald (1995) indicated that the number of available ESL courses was beginning to lag behind the demand for such courses. Ellis (1999) reports in a more recent study that 89 percent of community colleges responding to a nationwide survey noted that a majority of their students whose first language was not English came to the community college still needing work in language skills before taking credit courses with native speakers of English.

Community college ESL programs fall into several categories. In academic ESL programs, which usually offer institutional credit[1] and charge the standard institutional tuition, some students are preparing to first complete an associate degree and then go on to a degree at a four-year school; others have the goal of completing a certificate or associate degree and then working in their field of study; still others want only to improve their skills in English before applying to another school or looking for a new job. In adult education ESL programs, which are often tuition-free and not for

The author would like to thank Laurie Cox, Sarah Hawker, Alexandra Heder, Kathy Judd, Linda Lehman, Ilona Leki, and Francis Noji for the information they contributed in e-mail correspondence during 2000 and 2001.

credit, students usually have more fundamental and functional goals related to survival (shopping, renting an apartment, managing the health care system) or vocational matters (filling out a job application, learning job-related vocabulary).

Given the need for ESL at the community college and the wide variety of program and course formats now in place, what issues currently confront the field? This chapter explores some long-standing concerns along with more recent issues in community college ESL instruction: the diversity of the ESL student population and the difficulty of measuring student outcomes, the organizational placement and structure of community college ESL programs, employment issues for and training of instructors, the newly defined Generation 1.5 population, and financial and funding concerns.

The Diverse Community College ESL Population

One feature of the ESL population in the community college that is easily recognized but not as easily measured or addressed is its diverse makeup. A small minority of ESL students at the community college are international students who come to the United States on student visas and plan to return to their home countries upon completion of their studies (Ellis, 1999). These students are usually well educated in their native languages, have met a TOEFL score requirement set by the individual institution, and were it not for the need for further language study, would be well prepared for college-level work.

The majority of ESL students at the community college are refugees and immigrants (Ellis, 1999). Within this population are some students who, like international students, have been well educated in their native languages, but there are many who have not. Some have briefly attended U.S. high schools and can get along well in their daily lives in English, whereas others enter the community college with little or no English proficiency. Some community college ESL students plan on continuing their education beyond ESL, perhaps at a four-year institution, but others come to the community college for English instruction only. In addition, community colleges are also called on to provide ESL instruction off campus, for workers at local businesses. These individualized, usually noncredit programs tend to focus on elements of the English language that employers feel their workers need to succeed at their jobs and perhaps move up in the company. Other life skills or academic language needs are usually not a part of these programs.

How, then, in light of this diversity of needs and goals, is ESL student success to be measured? One point of agreement in the field is that defining, measuring, and documenting the success of ESL students is a complex and difficult task that has rarely been attempted outside of individual institutions (Ignash, 1995). Although retention may be the easiest statistic to gather, retention, especially in adult, noncredit, nonacademic education, is probably not an accurate measure of overall success.

Questions that look beyond retention, focusing on the achievement of real student goals, will provide more accurate measures of success. For instance, did the student who attended classes for only ten weeks leave the ESL program because she acquired enough English to get an entry-level job or because the program wasn't meeting her needs? Is a student leaving after one semester in an academic program because he has successfully raised his TOEFL score enough in one semester at the community college to transfer or because the program schedule is not compatible with his work and family obligations? Is the ESL program in need of improvement if students have to repeat courses, or is repetition of course levels simply reflective of the very nature of language learning? The design and implementation of accurate and useful short- and long-term research on the success of students in community college ESL remains a critical challenge to the profession.

ESL Programs: Finding a Home

Just as the diversity of ESL student populations presents a complex set of challenges in measuring success, the position or home of ESL within institutions offers similar challenges to the understanding of what works best for ESL students. At the community college, ESL may be housed in developmental education departments, English departments, foreign language departments, separate ESL departments, or adult education programs that are often tuition-free, basic-skills programs. Community colleges may sort ESL students into different programs housed in different areas of the college using criteria such as students' previous education, entering English language level, or educational goals.

In addition, student assessment and course placement procedures and policies differ widely from college to college. While one college might use a holistic writing assessment instrument to place ESL students into their initial courses and monitor students' subsequent progress, a college in a bordering district might use a discrete-point grammar test for the same purposes. Some colleges require that students enroll in certain levels of ESL, based on assessment results, while others leave that decision to the students. These differences significantly complicate the implementation of comparative studies of student and program success.

The availability of grant money and student financial aid restrictions can play a role in determining the structure and home of ESL programs and the policies that guide them. For instance, at Truman College in Chicago, three of six levels of academic ESL were moved to the adult education program, not because it necessarily made sense pedagogically, but because the college was under pressure from granting agencies to reserve student grant money for transfer-credit-bearing courses.

Although the wide range of program options in ESL offers flexibility for students, it also presents an important and exciting challenge for future research (Tichenor, 1994; Kuo, 1999, 2000). To date, there has not been a comprehensive study of the relationship of student outcomes to the organization and the position of ESL programs within an institution, but there are numerous questions that should be addressed. For instance, do ESL programs housed in English departments integrate students more effectively into the college and address academic ESL needs more directly, or do these programs lump ESL students with remedial students who may have very different course and program needs? Do programs that are organized by ESL students' previous education track students and limit future academic or vocational study? Do programs that include both international students and immigrants and refugees benefit or hinder the progress of either group?

As the pressure for accountability in education grows and as funding tightens, questions regarding the relationship of organizational structure to student success will need to be answered.

Employment and Training of ESL Professionals

In a recent informal survey of subscribers to the Community College ESL listserv (eslcc@hcc.Hawaii.edu), employment issues ranked high on ESL professionals' lists of concerns. The literature also supports this view. The reliance on part-time instructors (sometimes the *only* paid professionals in an ESL program) and the disrespect and second-class status many perceive they receive at their institutions are important issues for ESL professionals (Haworth, 1998; Ellis, 1999; Henrichsen and Savova, 2000). Part-time instructors in ESL, like those in other areas, are low-paid, often work at several institutions, and may have substantial commutes as they move from one college to another.

Even when ESL instructors are hired on a full-time basis, they are often not on a tenure track, in part because many ESL courses offer neither institutional nor transfer or degree credit (Haworth, 1998). For example, it is not uncommon for a coordinator of an established ESL program to work under a term-by-term adjunct contract instead of being on a permanent tenure-track one.

In addition, because ESL is a "skills" as opposed to a "content" field at the community college, many content-area colleagues view the field as less demanding and less rigorous than content fields or as something that anyone who speaks English can teach with little or no training. However, the ability to teach language skills involves more than the ability to produce and understand language. For instance, the ability to speak the language is not adequate preparation for the teaching of the rules for the various pronunciations of the letter *s* in words like *chairs* (/z/), *chats* (/s/), and *chalices* (/iz/) or for the physical manipulations needed to produce these distinct sounds.

It is often difficult for adult education programs to find highly qualified ESL instructors. Informal conversations with colleagues and a review of ESL job sites show that a master's in linguistics is the preferred degree for adult education ESL programs, but related bachelor's degrees are also accepted. These programs often have a particularly difficult time finding and keeping good instructors because academic programs tend to pay more and offer what some believe to be higher status and more stable employment than adult education programs. It is particularly difficult for company-based ESL programs to find qualified teachers who are skilled in the teaching of English and who possess the requisite industry knowledge.

Although there is general consensus in the literature about the conditions just described, a long-lasting solution that takes funding constraints into account has not been reached. Still, many observers contend there is a need to elevate ESL to the status granted other disciplines at the community college, with the appropriate funding base and commitment to full-time, tenure-track faculty. Perhaps one way to reinforce the advocacy for these changes is to engage in more formal research on how part-time to full-time teacher ratios affect student success in ESL. Do community college ESL programs with higher proportions of full-time teachers produce better student outcomes? How do ESL programs effectively retain, evaluate, and support their teachers? How does the lack of in-depth teacher training in many adult education programs affect student outcomes? These are complex research questions that could lead to important changes in both policy and practice.

Generation 1.5

"Generation 1.5" is a designation that reflects a pressing concern frequently addressed among community college ESL professionals. The term was first used in the late 1980s to describe immigrants who fit the description of neither first-generation nor second-generation Americans (Rumbaut and Ima, 1988). Generation 1.5 students are U.S.-educated ESL students. They usually arrive in the United States in their preteen or early teen years and acquire at least some education in U.S. high schools and possibly middle schools. By the time they arrive at the community college, they are often very fluent in and comfortable with informal spoken English. Yet their spoken language, though smooth and effortless, often reflects fossilized language errors. In other words, their day-to-day language is fluent but inaccurately so. Spoken language usually flows easily, without the pauses and discomfort that second-language learners often exhibit, and often includes idiomatic expressions that are common to native speakers. However, grammar and pronunciation consistently contain second-language errors. For example, in a recent advising session, a Generation 1.5 student said the following: "I want that I study computers only. The English classes, they doesn't help me and they're a pain." This utterance is understandable and contains the colloquial expression "a pain," but the grammatical errors are obvious.

Regarding writing, study skills, and the general knowledge one expects of a high school graduate, Generation 1.5 students are often ill prepared for college courses. Their (first-language) education had been interrupted by their pressing need both to learn spoken English and to become integrated into the high school or middle school community. Their academic skills, including reading, writing, critical thinking, and general knowledge, are often weak. In some respects, then, they are similar to traditional college-age remedial students and could benefit from some of the same programs and courses designed for native speakers of English. However, Generation 1.5 students are not native English speakers, and their second-language issues are often distinct from those of native English speakers. In particular, their grammar and pronunciation difficulties are not commonly addressed in remedial courses designed for native speakers, nor are most instructors of remedial English trained in these areas.

Still, traditional community college ESL classes haven't been designed to meet the needs of Generation 1.5 students, so most ESL classes are far from a perfect fit. Generation 1.5 students do not come to the community college for adult education ESL courses, as they often want to pursue a post-secondary education. However, Harklau, Siegal, and Losey (1999) note that academic college-level ESL pedagogy and materials are geared toward students who have recently arrived in the United States as adults, often with sophisticated educational backgrounds. For example, information on American culture is an integral part of the curriculum, understanding of formal grammar instruction is expected, and general world knowledge is assumed to be high. The usual framework and curriculum, then, of post-secondary academic ESL courses do not serve the needs of U.S.-educated ESL students.

Also, members of the Generation 1.5 student population are averse to placement in ESL. They often resent being put in the same category as new immigrants and become bored with instruction in U.S. culture. They become frustrated with formal grammar instruction, as this requires a level of metacognitive language skills with which they are unfamiliar and uncomfortable. Further, many Generation 1.5 students see an ESL placement as a step backward, as many had already advanced out of ESL in high school, leading to resentment of college policies toward them.

Statistics about the number of Generation 1.5 students at community colleges nationwide are not readily available, and individual institutions may have only recently begun to compile these statistics; however, it seems clear that the numbers are growing. For example, during the fall 2000 term at Kapiolani Community College in Honolulu, more than 50 percent of the ESL student population had attended high school in the United States, presenting that program with great challenges. Many miles and weather systems away, at William Rainey Harper College near Chicago, the Generation 1.5 population grew enough for the ESL program to offer special sections of reading and writing courses for students who fall into the Generation 1.5 category. Harper College also sponsored in 2000 a well-attended symposium at which area high schools and community colleges met to explore Generation 1.5 concerns. Although no one path was agreed on by attendees to best serve this group of students, points of consensus were that the number of Generation 1.5 students at the local high schools and community colleges was rising quickly and that their needs were not being met by the more traditional ESL curriculum.

Although Generation 1.5 students are present in four-year institutions, it is likely, because of this group's need for both remediation and ESL study and because of various economic and cultural constraints, that community colleges will be their primary source for their beginning postsecondary education. The community college is faced, then, with questions about how to best serve this population. How are these students to be identified accurately and fairly? Is the Generation 1.5 student best served by an ESL program, a remedial program, or a new program that combines ESL language study with remediation? Is a one-on-one tutoring or support approach the best strategy? What pedagogical approaches work best? How can high schools and community colleges work together to better prepare these students for college? Do separate programs for Generation 1.5 lead to better student outcomes? If so, how will these students be fairly and accurately assessed and placed? Should the overall ESL curriculum be changed to better serve these students, and if it is, will this have a negative impact on other groups of ESL students? Finally, how does the Generation 1.5 students' resentment at still being considered "ESL" affect their retention and performance in college?

"Show Me the Money"

Institutional-credit ESL programs encounter many of the same financial issues as other community college courses and programs. Community college budgets vary from district to district and must balance competing needs for instructors, space, and services. And tuition-free adult education ESL programs struggle with a wider variety of funding dilemmas.

First, funding of adult education ESL is often tied to politics, laws, and fast-changing public opinion. For example, in the late 1980s, funding for community-based ESL classes became abundant under the Immigration Reform and Control Act of 1986 (commonly referred to as "amnesty funding"). Community college adult education ESL programs benefited greatly from these dollars. However, this money was no longer available in the early 1990s, leaving many community college programs with tough decisions about how to spend the money that remained from other sources. For instance, Kurzet (1997) tells of the crisis Portland Community College faced when it was suddenly forced to cut courses and faculty by approximately 50 percent after losing amnesty funds. In rebuilding, the college paid great attention to the balance between maintaining a quality program and serving a large number of students.

The days of amnesty funding are gone, but funding and governance instabilities remain. For instance, state mechanisms for managing funds and programs can go through significant changes. One current example of this is in Illinois, where the governance and funding of adult education have been transferred from the Illinois State Board of Education (ISBE) to the Illinois Community College Board (ICCB), primarily because the majority of students taking advantage of adult education programs in the state are enrolled in community college, not high school, programs. This transfer between agencies is logical, and it is not expected that the amount of money available for ESL will decrease. Indeed, funding and services to programs and instructors might even increase. Still, changes in record keeping and reporting will be taxing for some programs, and any shifts in the funding and governance system bring concerns about the smooth implementation of even the best plans.

Another issue related to funding is the use of volunteer teachers and tutors in adult education ESL. The lack of adequate or stable funding has led many programs to rely heavily on volunteer teachers. While individual community service is, of course, admirable and personally rewarding, it can seriously strain any ESL program. Volunteers often work for only a short time and can leave suddenly. Furthermore, volunteers do not usually have the pedagogical or linguistics background of trained ESL teachers. On the positive side, because volunteers often work one on one or with small groups, student learning is generally very high. In addition, volunteers can provide one-on-one support to new arrivals in nonlanguage areas that a classroom teacher might not address.

Assessing the impact of various funding and governance mechanisms and examining the best roles for volunteers in community college ESL programs are important research and program challenges.

Conclusion

Postsecondary ESL courses, especially at the community college level, meet a growing need and serve many students successfully; still, many research questions remain. Although the issues presented here are not the only challenges faced by the profession, they present a glimpse of some of the more pressing concerns of ESL at the community college today.

Note

1. *Institutional credit* refers to in-house credit that counts only for calculating tuition and applying academic rules and penalties at individual institutions. *Transfer credit* refers to credit that most other community colleges and four-year schools will apply toward their own degree requirements.

References

Ellis, P. "Standard Bearer: Report on the Community College Employment Standards Task Force." *TESOL Matters,* June-July 1999.

Fitzgerald, N. *ESL Instruction in Adult Education: Findings from a National Evaluation.* Washington, D.C.: National Clearinghouse for ESL Literacy Education, 1995.

Harklau, L., Siegal, M., and Losey, K. M. "Linguistically Diverse Students and College Writing: What Is Equitable and Appropriate?" In L. Harklau, K. M. Losey, and M. Siegal (eds.), *Generation 1.5 Meets College Composition: Issues in the Teaching of Writing to U.S.-Educated Learners of ESL.* Mahwah, N.J.: Erlbaum, 1999.

Haworth, K. "Teachers of English as a Second Language Strive for More Recognition in Academe." *Chronicle of Higher Education,* July 31, 1998, p. A7.

Henrichsen, L. E., and Savova, L. P. "International and Historical Perspectives on the Preparation of ESOL Teachers." *TESOL Journal,* 2000, 9(3), 3–4.

Ignash, J. M. "Encouraging ESL Student Persistence: The Influence of Policy on Curricular Design." *Community College Review,* 1995, 23(3), 17–34.

Kuo, E. "English as a Second Language in the Community College Curriculum." In G. Schuyler (ed.), *Trends in Community College Curriculum.* New Directions for Community Colleges, no. 108. San Francisco: Jossey-Bass, 1999.

Kuo, E. "English as a Second Language: Program Approaches at Community Colleges." 2000. (ED 447 859)

Kurzet, R. "Quality Versus Quantity in the Delivery of Developmental Programs for ESL Students." In J. M. Ignash (ed.), *Implementing Effective Policies for Remedial and Developmental Education.* New Directions for Community Colleges, no. 100. San Francisco: Jossey-Bass, 1997.

Rumbaut, R. G., and Ima, K. *The Adaptation of Southeast Asian Refugee Youth: A Comparative Study.* San Diego, Calif.: San Diego State University, 1988. (ED 299 372)

Schuyler, G. "A Historical and Contemporary View of the Community College Curriculum." In G. Schuyler (ed.), *Trends in Community College Curriculum.* New Directions for Community Colleges, no. 108. San Francisco: Jossey-Bass, 1999.

Tichenor, S. "Community Colleges and Teaching English as a Second Language: Serving the Limited English Proficient." *Community College Review,* 1994, 22(3), 55–67.

AMY J. BLUMENTHAL *has taught ESL for more than two decades. She is a professor of English and an ESL specialist at Oakton Community College in Des Plaines, Illinois.*

*Assessment of student learning outcomes has emerged as
a major issue for higher education in terms of
accreditation, accountability, and performance indicators
and performance funding. This chapter reviews the
literature concerning assessment of student learning
outcomes in general education, transfer programs, career
and occupational programs, remedial and developmental
courses and programs, noncredit and continuing
education offerings, and affective and noncognitive
outcomes, as well as the use of assessment results.*

Assessing Student Learning Outcomes

Jeffrey A. Seybert

Effective assessment of student learning outcomes is a major issue for higher
education. Numerous national meetings, books and articles, workshops, and
speeches have addressed it. All of the regional accrediting agencies have
incorporated some level of effectiveness or student learning outcomes
assessment activities into their criteria for accreditation and reaffirmation
of accreditation. In addition, a majority of the states have also mandated
some form of effectiveness assessment activity (Erwin, 1991). Thus unlike
many initiatives and reforms in higher education that tend to arise and then
disappear relatively quickly, the assessment movement seems to be gaining
rather than losing strength.

There is a substantial and growing body of literature focused on assessment, the majority of which deals with four-year colleges and universities.
Though assessment in community colleges is in some ways similar to that
in four-year colleges and universities, there are also major differences.
Community college missions are typically much broader, including career
and occupational programs, remedial and developmental coursework, and
various other educational offerings in addition to traditional liberal arts
and sciences transfer programs. Community college students are much
more diverse demographically than their four-year counterparts (Bean and
Metzner, 1985), and they have diverse educational objectives. Many already
have a bachelor's degree or higher (Phillippe and Valiga, 2000). Thus assessment measures common to four-year colleges and universities (graduation
rates, for example) are much less appropriate for community colleges. This
chapter addresses assessment of student learning in the major academic
areas common to the vast majority of community colleges: general education, transfer programs, career and occupational programs, remedial and

developmental courses and programs, and noncredit and continuing education offerings. Other important topics related to student learning, such as affective and noncognitive outcomes and use of assessment results, are discussed briefly.

General Education Outcomes

Community colleges typically require degree-seeking (and in some cases, certificate-seeking) students to take courses in several core academic areas in addition to courses in their declared major or program. These general education requirements may include areas such as mathematics, oral and written communication, critical thinking and problem solving, technology, or diversity and multiculturalism. Often requirements are met by taking courses in traditional academic subject areas such as humanities, science, and social science in addition to English and mathematics. Thus measurement of student achievement of this general education core is a major component in colleges' overall efforts to assess student learning, and it has received considerable attention in the literature.

Alfred, Ewell, Hudgins, and McClenney (1999) identified two broad areas that should be involved in the assessment of general education competence: critical literacy skills (communication, critical thinking, problem solving, and interpersonal skills) and citizenship skills (community involvement, multicultural understanding, and leadership). They also suggested methodologies and data sources for assessment of these skills including standardized tests, authentic performance-based methodologies, alumni follow-up surveys, and portfolios. Likewise, Seybert (1994a) suggested several methodologies appropriate for assessment of general education, including standardized and locally developed tests, student portfolios, final projects, and capstone experiences and courses.

Standardized tests are used to assess student knowledge of core general education areas in many community colleges in spite of the numerous challenges of doing so. Several standardized tests appropriate for community college students are available, including the ACT CAAP, ACT COMP, College BASE, and ETS Academic Profile (Nichols, 1989; Seybert, 1998). A variety of other methodologies have also been used to assess students' knowledge of general education topics. Klassen (1984) assessed students' critical thinking ability using pre- and posttesting with the Watson-Glaser Critical Thinking Appraisal in a longitudinal study of returning adult students who completed the "Weekend Social Science Option" at a large community college. Seybert and O'Hara (1997) described a performance-based institutional portfolio model developed to assess general education at Johnson County Community College in Kansas. Samples of student work produced in classes are evaluated by interdisciplinary faculty teams using holistic scoring rubrics.

Faculty and staff at Oakton Community College in Illinois (Bers, 2000; Bers, Davis, and Mittler, 2001) have developed a cross-disciplinary approach to assessment of general education. Students respond to questions administered in courses from a variety of disciplines with high numbers of enrollees who have earned 30 or more credit hours. Students' answers are scored by faculty teams using holistic scoring rubrics. Their performance is evaluated at a high-pass, low-pass, or no-pass level. Finally, faculty at Columbus State Community College in Ohio have developed a unique two-course sequence: the Freshman Experience course to inform students about general education requirements, expected outcomes, and faculty expectations and to provide them with the necessary tools to plan and be successful in their academic experience; and the Capstone Experience course to assess student performance on those outcomes (Hunt, 2000). All of these examples of assessment of general education outcomes used direct measurement of student achievement.

These types of performance-based assessment methodologies are increasingly gaining acceptance for assessment of general education learning outcomes, in place of standardized tests. They have the advantage of being much more diagnostic and prescriptive in assisting faculty as they attempt to improve curriculum and pedagogy to enhance student learning.

Transfer Outcomes

The transfer function was the cornerstone component of the community college mission when two-year colleges were first created as junior colleges (Brint and Karabel, 1989), and it remains an important facet of the modern community college mission today. It is important to note here that the majority of community colleges measure transfer student learning outcomes only indirectly, through follow-up studies of those students after they have transferred to a four-year college or university. These studies typically include surveys of the former students, academic performance data supplied by the senior institution (or from a statewide database maintained by a state board of regents or a similar agency), and possibly focus groups with former students sometime after transfer.

Alfred, Ewell, Hudgins, and McClenney (1999) identified three core indicators to assess the transfer function: the number of students who transfer in a given year, transfer rate (defined as the percentage of an identified cohort of transfer students who subsequently do, in fact, transfer), and student academic performance after transfer. Other authors have suggested additional measures to assess the transfer function, including surveys of former transfer students (Seybert, 1994b), calculation of a national or statewide transfer rate by aggregating transfer data from as many individual colleges as possible (Nichols, 1989; Preston and Bailey, 1993), and the transferability of courses based on articulation agreements with the transfer institution (Calhoun, 1991).

Seybert (1993b) posed four questions to guide the assessment effort: Do transfer students accomplish their community college educational objective? How do they evaluate their community college experiences? Do they actually transfer, and if so, at what rates? Do they succeed at four-year colleges and universities? In a similar model, Carroll (1990) first identified the various types of transfer students (traditional, career preparation, reverse, and casual), discussed the different community college programs those students might engage, posed thirteen questions to guide assessment of transfer, and suggested multiple data sources to provide answers to the questions.

A novel approach to assessment of transfer has been suggested by Quanty, Dixon, and Ridley (1998). They noted that traditional transfer assessment techniques track particular students from the community college to their transfer institution. What they proposed in their Course-Based Model of Transfer Success (CMBTS), however, shifts that focus to how well students who complete course prerequisites at a community college perform in specific courses, compared to students who complete the prerequisites at the receiving senior institution. The emphasis is on how well courses prepare students. Initial results of the model demonstrated that students who complete prerequisites at a community college performed at a level at least equivalent to students who complete those same prerequisites at the receiving institution.

A large, statewide transfer assessment study conducted by the Johnson County Community College Office of Institutional Research in Kansas (1992) produced several interesting results. The project involved nearly eleven thousand students who transferred from any of the nineteen community colleges in Kansas to any of the seven public universities in the state. Major findings indicated that academic progress (measured by cumulative hours earned toward a degree) and performance (measured by cumulative GPA) of the community college and native university students studied were essentially the same, even though the former community college students initially suffered the well-documented temporary posttransfer drop in GPA known as transfer shock (see, for example, Diaz, 1992; Keeley and House, 1993; Preston, 1993). However, native university students persisted and graduated at higher rates than their community college transfer counterparts, a finding similar to that reported several times in the literature (see, for example, Dougherty, 1987, 1992).

Career and Occupational Outcomes

Since the mid-twentieth century, career and occupational programs have assumed increasing importance as one of the major mission components of community colleges. In fact, in many colleges, enrollment in these programs has equaled or surpassed that in the more traditional transfer programs. Thus it is generally agreed that assessment of career and occupational outcomes is an important component of an overall program to assess student learning outcomes.

Measurement of career and occupational outcomes in community colleges is unique in that it is the only major set of outcomes widely assessed using both direct and indirect measures of student achievement. Indirect measures, such as follow-up surveys of former career program students, surveys of their current employers, data regarding placement rates of former career program students in the workforce, and employment and wage and salary data from state labor department databases, are very common (see, for example, Seybert, 1994b; Alfred, Ewell, Hudgins, and McClenney, 1999; Stevenson, Walleri, and Japely, 1985; Walleri and Seybert, 1993).

There are also numerous reports in the literature describing direct measurement of student learning outcomes in career programs. In fields where they are available, standardized licensing examinations provide a valuable way to directly assess student achievement (Alfred, Ewell, Hudgins, and McClenney, 1999). For example, such tests are available in most allied health professions (nursing, dental hygiene, paramedic, medical laboratory technician, radiologic technology, and respiratory therapy) (Calhoun, 1991). A specific example of the use of such a standardized test was cited by Bowyer (1996). She reported that on average, nursing students at Dyersburg State Community College in Tennessee scored lower than passing scores on a specific National League for Nursing (NLN) achievement test. As a result, the nursing curriculum was modified to include more of the material targeted by that specific test, and subsequent student scores improved.

There are also reports involving novel approaches to direct assessment of student outcomes. Goldman (1999) described use of a "structured simulated clinical examination" (SSCE) to improve curriculum and student learning in the nursing program at Sinclair Community College in Ohio. The SSCE uses a case study format, patient actors, and observation of student performance by faculty raters using standardized rating scales.

Finally, Seybert (1990, 1993a, 1993c) has outlined a comprehensive model to assess career and occupational student learning outcomes using both direct and indirect measures of student achievement as just outlined. The 1990 paper provides a more detailed description of such a model and includes seventeen major questions and concomitant sets of data sources to answer those questions. For a variety of reasons, including the fact that there are multiple available direct and indirect measures of career student achievement, community colleges have made greater progress in assessment of career and occupational student learning outcomes than in any other major outcomes category.

Remedial and Developmental Outcomes

As with career and occupational outcomes, remedial and developmental outcomes have been measured both directly and indirectly. Alfred, Ewell, Hudgins, and McClenney (1999), for example, have proposed an indirect measure, student success in subsequent, related coursework. Several authors have reported results of remedial and developmental assessment efforts using a variety of additional direct and indirect measures, including completion of the developmental course sequence, overall academic performance and progress, and graduation rates (Seybert and Soltz, 1996; Walleri, 1996; Walleri and Seybert, 1993).

Quinley (1990) proposed a comprehensive model to assess the outcomes of remedial and developmental courses and programs. Included in this model was a series of eleven major questions along with concomitant data sources designed to provide information regarding the questions. The questions and data sources involve both direct and indirect measurement of remedial and developmental student learning outcomes and as such can serve as a suitable foundation for a model to assess these outcomes.

Noncredit and Continuing Education Outcomes

Providing noncredit continuing education and community service courses and programs constitutes an important and growing component of the overall mission of most two-year colleges. In fact, in some colleges, noncredit and continuing education head counts may exceed those for credit students. These programs and courses cover a wide range of personal interest, community service, cultural, business and industry training, continuing professional education, and other offerings of various formats and lengths.

The need to assess the outcomes of these courses and programs has been recognized by a few authors (for example, Banta, 1999). Cosgrove (1990) has proposed a comprehensive set of questions to guide assessment efforts in this area, along with a set of suggested data sources to provide data to answer the questions. More recently, Seybert (1995) has also suggested a multimethod approach to assessment of noncredit and continuing education outcomes, including noncredit student course evaluation forms, participant and employer follow-up evaluation surveys, and short surveys and focus groups. Licensure renewal rates for participants in mandated continuing professional education courses are an important index of the outcomes of this type of noncredit offering. Clearly, all of these methodologies measure the learning outcomes of noncredit or continuing education programs and courses only indirectly. More work is necessary to directly assess the outcomes of this growing component of the community college mission.

Affective and Noncognitive Outcomes

All of the categories of student learning outcomes discussed previously have dealt with the cognitive domain. Many community colleges, however, also indicate in their mission statements that students should achieve a variety of outcomes in the affective and noncognitive domain.

Examples of these outcomes include citizenship skills, understanding and appreciation of multiculturalism and diversity, self-confidence, value and goal clarification, moral development, and tolerance (Seybert, 1998). To date, however, there have been very few reports in the literature of assessment of these types of outcomes in community colleges, and several authors have commented on the need for assessing this complex set of outcomes (for example, Alfred, Ewell, Hudgins, and McClenney, 1999; Pascarella and Terenzini, 1991; Seybert, 1994b). Given the frequency with which such outcomes appear and are emphasized in community college mission and values statements, it is clear that much work remains to be done to assess whether students are actually acquiring those skills and abilities.

Use of Assessment Results

It is widely agreed that the ultimate purpose of assessment lies not in actual assessment techniques and methodologies themselves but in the use of assessment results to improve teaching, learning, and delivery of services to students (for example, Banta and Associates, 1993; Banta, Lund, Black, and Oblander, 1996; Seybert, 1998). In fact, if assessment results are not used for improvement, the time, effort, and resources used to implement assessment processes and obtain assessment results are wasted. Examples of effective use of assessment results have been described for several of the works cited. Additional examples can be found in Banta (1999); Banta, Lund, Black, and Oblander (1996); and Banta and Associates (1993).

Conclusion

This chapter includes references to much of the extant literature concerning assessment of student learning outcomes in community colleges. It includes sources that provide practical approaches to assessment that would assist both those interested in studying community colleges and practitioners looking for proven, feasible techniques to implement as a part of overall assessment efforts on campuses.

It is clear from this review that assessment of student learning outcomes in community colleges has been implemented to a greater degree for some outcomes categories than for others. In general, for example, the literature seems to indicate that institutions have made greatest progress in assessment of career and occupational outcomes. Somewhat less, though significant, assessment work has been accomplished for transfer and general education outcomes. Relatively little assessment work is evident and much remains to be accomplished in assessment of remedial and developmental, noncredit and continuing education, and affective and noncognitive outcomes.

In addition to these areas that have been addressed (to greater or lesser degrees), there are also a variety of issues around assessment that have yet to be considered in any systematic way in community colleges. For example, how do we assess students from multicultural backgrounds or students with physical or learning disabilities? How do we assess learning outcomes for students participating in distance learning and other asynchronous pedagogies? How do we motivate students to do good work on assessments that don't count directly in their course grades or are not required for graduation? Are there concrete, effective incentives to get students to take assessment seriously? Is it feasible for institutions that share students (between which there are numerous transfers) also to share assessment? Will community colleges (and higher education in general) be ultimately subjected to the high-stakes testing that's taking on so much importance in K–12? These and other similar issues have received very little, if any, attention in the literature on assessment in community colleges and may take on increasing importance as the assessment movement matures.

Assessment of student learning outcomes, and to a lesser extent of overall institutional effectiveness, has several major implications for community colleges. Among these are the relationship of assessment results to local and state accountability initiatives and statewide performance indicators and performance-based funding schemes. Perhaps the most salient and certainly the most immediate for most institutions, however, is the degree to which progress on assessment and use of assessment results will affect the institution's prospects for reaffirmation of regional accreditation. The North Central Association (NCA) Higher Learning Commission has, within the last two or three years, renewed and increased its decadelong emphasis on the importance of assessment as a cornerstone of the institutional self-study and accreditation process. Specifically, NCA has created an assessment matrix plotting levels of implementation against patterns of characteristics to assist institutions in evaluating their progress on implementation of comprehensive assessment of student learning outcomes and use of assessment results (Lopez, 2000, 2001). While not explicitly requiring use of the matrix in reaccreditation self-studies, it has a prominent place in the current NCA handbook and is widely used by NCA consultant evaluator teams as they evaluate institutions' worthiness for reaccreditation. Thus rather than fading away, like many of the initiatives and reforms in the recent history of higher education, assessment of student learning outcomes has become a major issue for colleges and universities in the twenty-first century.

References

Alfred, R., Ewell, P., Hudgins, J., and McClenney, K. *Core Indicators of Effectiveness for Community Colleges.* (2nd ed.) Washington, D.C.: Community College Press, 1999.

Banta, T. W. *Assessment in Community Colleges: Setting the Standard for Higher Education.* Boulder, Colo.: National Center for Higher Education Management Systems, 1999.

Banta, T. W., Lund, J. P., Black, K. E., and Oblander, F. W. (eds.). *Assessment in Practice: Putting Principles to Work on College Campuses.* San Francisco: Jossey-Bass, 1996.

Banta, T. W., and Associates. *Making a Difference: Outcomes of a Decade of Assessment in Higher Education.* San Francisco: Jossey-Bass, 1993.

Bean, J. P., and Metzner, B. S. "A Conceptual Model of Nontraditional Student Attrition." *Review of Educational Research,* 1985, *55,* 485–540.

Bers, T. H. "Assessing the Achievement of General Education Objectives: Second Year of a Collegewide Approach and Lessons Learned." *Journal of Applied Research in the Community College,* 2000, *7,* 101–113.

Bers, T. H., Davis, B. D., and Mittler, M. L. "Assessing the Achievement of General Education Objectives in the Community College: A Project Across the Disciplines." *Assessment Update,* 2001, *13*(3), 6–7, 13.

Bowyer, K. A. "Efforts to Continually Improve a Nursing Program." In T. W. Banta, J. P. Lund, K. E. Black, and F. W. Oblander (eds.), *Assessment in Practice: Putting Principles to Work on College Campuses.* San Francisco: Jossey-Bass, 1996.

Brint, S., and Karabel, J. *The Diverted Dream: Community Colleges and the Promise of Educational Opportunity in America, 1900–1985.* New York: Oxford University Press, 1989.

Calhoun, H. "Implementing Institutional Effectiveness at Two-Year Colleges." In J. O. Nichols (ed.), *A Practitioner's Handbook for Institutional Effectiveness and Student Outcomes Assessment Implementation.* New York: Agathon Press, 1991.

Carroll, S. "The Transfer Mission." In D. Doucette and B. Hughes (eds.), *Assessing Institutional Effectiveness in Community Colleges.* Laguna Hills, Calif.: League for Innovation in the Community College, 1990.

Cosgrove, J. "The Continuing Education and Community Service Mission." In D. Doucette and B. Hughes (eds.), *Assessing Institutional Effectiveness in Community Colleges.* Laguna Hills, Calif.: League for Innovation in the Community College, 1990.

Diaz, P. E. "Effects of Transfer on Academic Performance of Community College Students at the Four-Year Institution." *Community/Junior College Quarterly of Research and Practice,* 1992, *16*(3), 279–291.

Dougherty, K. "The Effects of Community Colleges: Aid or Hindrance to Socioeconomic Attainment?" *Sociology of Education,* 1987, *60,* 86–103.

Dougherty, K. "Community Colleges and Baccalaureate Attainment." *Journal of Higher Education,* 1992, *63,* 188–214.

Erwin, T. D. *Assessing Student Learning and Development: A Guide to the Principles, Goals, and Methods of Determining College Outcomes.* San Francisco: Jossey-Bass, 1991.

Goldman, G. "Simulated Performance Assessment in a Community College Nursing Program." *Assessment Update,* 1999, *11*(3), 12–15.

Hudgins, J. L., Kitchings, D. A., and Williams, S. K. "Laying the Foundation for Effectiveness Through Assessment." In T. W. Banta, J. P. Lund, K. E. Black, and F. W. Oblander (eds.), *Assessment in Practice: Putting Principles to Work on College Campuses.* San Francisco: Jossey-Bass, 1996.

Hunt, S. "Using a Capstone Course to Assess General Education Outcomes." *Assessment Update,* 2000, *12*(2), 8–9.

Johnson County Community College Office of Institutional Research. *Students Moving from the Community Colleges to the Regents Institutions in the State of Kansas.* Overland Park, Kans.: Johnson County Community College, 1992.

Keeley, E. J., III, and House, J. D. "Transfer Shock Revisited: A Longitudinal Study of Transfer Academic Performance." Paper presented at the annual forum of the Association for Institutional Research, Chicago, May 1993.

Klassen, P. "Changes in Personal Orientation and Critical Thinking Among Adults Returning to School Through Weekend College: An Alternative Evaluation." *Innovative Higher Education,* 1984, *8,* 55–67.

Lopez, C. L. "Making Progress on Assessment: Using the 'Levels of Implementation' to Improve Student Learning." Paper presented at the Pacific Rim Conference on Higher Education Planning and Assessment, Hilo, Hawaii, June 2000.

Lopez, C. L. "Assessment of Student Learning in Context: What We Know; What We Are Learning." Paper presented at the Kansas Statewide Assessment Workshop, Hutchinson, Kans., Apr. 2001.

Nichols, J. O. *Institutional Effectiveness and Outcomes Assessment Implementation on Campus: A Practitioner's Handbook.* New York: Agathon Press, 1989.

Pascarella, E. T., and Terenzini, P. T. *How College Affects Students: Findings and Insights from Twenty Years of Research.* San Francisco: Jossey-Bass, 1991.

Phillippe, K. A., and Valiga, M. J. *Faces of the Future: A Portrait of America's Community College Students.* Washington, D.C.: Community College Press, 2000.

Preston, D. L. "Interfacing Two-Year and Four-Year Transcripts for Transfer Students." Paper presented at the annual forum of the Association for Institutional Research, Chicago, May 1993.

Preston, D. L., and Bailey, R. R. "How Can We Track Students from Two-Year to Four-year Institutions?" Paper presented at the annual forum of the Association for Institutional Research, Chicago, May 1993.

Quanty, M., Dixon, R., and Ridley, D. "A New Paradigm for Evaluating Transfer Success." *Assessment Update,* 1998, *10*(2), 12–13.

Quinley, J. "The Basic Skills and Developmental Education Mission." In D. Doucette and B. Hughes (eds.), *Assessing Institutional Effectiveness in Community Colleges.* Laguna Hills, Calif.: League for Innovation in the Community College, 1990.

Seybert, J. A. "The Career Preparation Mission." In D. Doucette and B. Hughes (eds.), *Assessing Institutional Effectiveness in Community Colleges.* Laguna Hills, Calif.: League for Innovation in the Community College, 1990.

Seybert, J. A. "Assessment of Career and Occupational Education." *Assessment Update,* 1993a, *5*(6), 14–15.

Seybert, J. A. "Assessment of the Transfer Function." *Assessment Update,* 1993b, *5*(4), 13–15.

Seybert, J. A. "Making the Grade: Assessment Provides Focus for Vocational Programs." *Vocational Education Journal,* 1993c, *68*(2), 22–23, 49.

Seybert, J. A. "Assessing Student Learning." *Assessment Update,* 1994a, 6 (4), 8–9.

Seybert, J. A. "Assessment from a National Perspective: Where Are We, Really?" In T. H. Bers and M. L. Mittler (eds.), *Assessment and Testing: Myths and Realities.* New Directions for Community Colleges, no. 88. San Francisco: Jossey-Bass, 1994b.

Seybert, J. A. "Assessment of Non-Credit/Continuing Education and Community Service Programs and Courses." *Assessment Update,* 1995, 7(2), 12–13.

Seybert, J. A. "Assessment in Community Colleges: Lessons from the USA." In A. H. Styrdom and L.O.K. Lategan (eds.), *Introducing Community Colleges to South Africa.* Bloemfontein, South Africa: University of the Free State, 1998.

Seybert, J. A., and O'Hara, K. A. "Implementation of a Performance-Based Model for Assessment of General Education." *Assessment Update,* 1997, 9(4), 5–7.

Seybert, J. A., and Soltz, D. F. "Assessment of Developmental Programs." In T. W. Banta, J. P. Lund, K. E. Black, and F. W. Oblander (eds.), *Assessment in Practice: Putting Principles to Work on College Campuses.* San Francisco: Jossey-Bass, 1996.

Stevenson, M., Walleri, R. D., and Japely, S. M. "Designing Follow-Up Studies of Graduates and Former Students." In P. T. Ewell (ed.), *Assessing Educational Outcomes.* New Directions for Institutional Research, no. 47. San Francisco: Jossey-Bass, 1985.

Walleri, R. D. "A Ten-Year Effort to Assist Underprepared Students." In T. W. Banta, J. P. Lund, K. E. Black, and F. W. Oblander (eds.), *Assessment in Practice: Putting Principles to Work on College Campuses.* San Francisco: Jossey-Bass, 1996.

Walleri, R. D., and Seybert, J. A. "Demonstrating and Enhancing Community College Effectiveness." In T. W. Banta and Associates, *Making a Difference: Outcomes of a Decade of Assessment in Higher Education.* San Francisco: Jossey-Bass, 1993.

JEFFREY A. SEYBERT *is director of research, evaluation, and instructional development at Johnson County Community College in Overland Park, Kansas.*

In this chapter, the author identifies key challenges facing student services units in the community college: student diversity, a renewed focus on student success, and calls to demonstrate program effectiveness.

Challenges in Supporting Student Learning and Success Through Student Services

Terry E. Williams

Student services professionals are committed to student learning and development and to creating campus environments that support all students, regardless of their educational goals. These professionals are involved in teaching and learning, much of which occurs outside the formal classroom, and they form collaborative programs both inside and outside the college to address the diverse needs of students and to foster student success. Typically, student services functions include such areas as "admissions and registration, advising and course placement, assessment and testing, athletics, counseling, discipline, financial aid, orientation, job placement, retention, student activities and campus life, and services for special need students" (Culp, 1995, p. 35).

To perform their various functions effectively, student services staff in community colleges face numerous challenges, most of which cluster around three broad themes: challenges arising from the increasing diversity of students, the call for a renewed focus on student learning and success, and the need to demonstrate more clearly the benefits of the work of student services units for students and the institution.

The author acknowledges and thanks Lois Voigt, research assistant in the Department of Leadership, Foundations, and Counseling Psychology at the School of Education, Loyola University, Chicago, for her assistance in the preparation of this chapter.

Student Diversity

The population of students choosing to enroll at two-year colleges will continue to increase over the next few years and will mirror the increasing diversity of American society. This diversity presents complex challenges and opportunities not only for the design and delivery of student affairs programs but also for all programs and service units within the community college (Culp and Helfgot, 1998; Ender, Chand, and Thornton, 1996). Thanks to the special role of community colleges, which serve as low-cost, open-access institutions with missions designed to meet the comprehensive and diverse needs of their local communities, they attract significant numbers of students who represent a true cross section of their communities.

Today's community college students are increasingly diverse along intersecting dimensions that include gender, age, race and ethnicity, religion, disability, family history of college attendance, academic intentions, academic preparation, motivational levels, economic backgrounds, learning styles, part-time versus full-time enrollment status, commitments and obligations outside the college, and English-speaking ability (Ender, Chand, and Thornton, 1996).

Data from the National Center for Education Statistics (1998) confirm that the two-year sector enrolls larger proportions of racial and ethnic minority students than the four-year sector. In 1996, minority students comprised 32 percent of all two-year college enrollments, compared to 26 percent for all undergraduate enrollments in the four-year sector. Almost half of all African American and Asian and Pacific Islander students enrolled in higher education attend a two-year college, along with 56 percent of American Indian students and 61 percent of all Hispanic students. In fall 1997, women comprised a majority (58 percent) of students in community colleges. Fully 63 percent of women and 57 percent of men are of "nontraditional" age (twenty-two years or older). The majority are enrolled on a part-time basis (63 percent), and approximately half of all community college students work while they are enrolled (Phillippe and Patton, 2000).

Complex challenges and opportunities arise for student affairs staffs as a direct result of the tremendous diversity that is represented by the community college students they seek to serve. While Helfgot (1998) asserts that the arrival of increasing numbers of diverse students represents a "continuing wave of the unders—the underprepared, the underrepresented, the underachieving, the underclass" (p. 3), he cautions that not all students share the same needs, concerns, expectations, and aspirations.

Challenges arise for community colleges and their staffs because the students they serve are often "at risk," not only because many come to the campus academically underprepared but also because they often work thirty or more hours a week, have little financial or personal support from their families, are the first in their families to attend college, or may come to campus expecting to fail. Many of these students arrive on campus wrestling with the development of academic and social competence, autonomy, interpersonal relationships, sexual identity, and career, work, and lifestyle needs (Ortiz, 1995).

Despite the diversity in their backgrounds and their goals, many of these students share one characteristic: The community college is often their first foray into higher education. If no one at home has attended an institution of higher learning, family members are often unable to provide helpful guidance or advice on how to negotiate college successfully. Many students also receive little or no financial or even moral support for their educational goals and aspirations.

Proposed Solutions. Student affairs staff must be knowledgeable about their students and the diverse needs they bring to the campus (Marcus, 1999). This response requires a dual commitment to staff development by focusing on the recruitment of a diverse professional staff committed to working toward students' success and by enhancing staff understanding and appreciation for the differences among students through ongoing programs of staff development training. Student affairs staff should also be equipped and empowered to educate faculty and administrators about students' unique needs and expectations.

Another message found in the literature is that the design and delivery of student affairs programs must be flexible and adaptable, in keeping with the needs of diverse students arriving on the campus. Programs and services need to be offered in varying formats and at different times of the day and night. Holding an orientation program for new students will not serve students well if it is offered at times they are unable to attend, in formats that don't match their learning styles, or in a language that they cannot easily understand (Helfgot, 1998).

Many students arriving on the community college campus today need a wide range of student-centered support in order to be successful (Rendon, 1994). Programs are needed to orient all new students to the campus and its services in order to instill a sense of belonging in the college. Also needed are programs provide comprehensive academic support services, including advising and basic skills assessment, study skills development and tutoring support, career exploration, and financial assistance. The keys to responding to the diverse needs of students are to first understand what those needs include, then to design creative and flexible programs that address these needs, and finally to assess the effectiveness of those programs.

A Clear Mission: Focusing on Student Learning and Success

Student services staff in the community college must also meet the challenge of identifying a clear and focused mission that supports student learning and success. Having a clear and focused mission directs attention to the overarching goals of student services, and communicates to all student services staff and to the larger college community a commitment to a set of core beliefs and values: students and their success.

Helfgot (1998) and others (Elsner and Ames, 1983; Matson and Deegan, 1985) indicate that on many campuses, faculty, the administration, students, and even student services staff have not always had a clear understanding of the primary purpose of the student services division. These scholars note various attempts over the years by student affairs professionals and associations to articulate a clear vision for the role of student affairs units. At the national level, several statements of purpose and philosophy have been promulgated in an attempt to provide clarity and commitment within the student affairs profession to a set of core values, beliefs, and functions. Recent statements, in part, include *Good Practice in Student Affairs: Principles to Foster Student Learning* (Blimling and Whitt, 1999), *The Student Learning Imperative* (American College Personnel Association, 1996), and *Powerful Partnerships: A Shared Responsibility for Learning* (Joint Task Force, 1998). *The Student Learning Imperative,* in particular, has received a great deal of attention by asserting that the core mission of student affairs units is to complement the institution's mission, with student learning and development as the primary goals of their programs and services.

While the learning imperative resonates well with many student affairs staff, some individuals in the community college sector have been critical of certain assumptions behind this approach. For example, Helfgot (1998, p. 31) asserts that the framework for student learning outcomes "rests on assumptions about students that aren't always true." The document, he believes, posits that the realization of true student learning requires students and student services staff to interact in ways that more closely mirror the needs and characteristics of traditional students in higher education and not those of the typical nontraditional community college student. For example, many nontraditional community college students cannot devote the amount of time to cocurricular activities that the learning imperative suggests lead to enhanced student learning.

Given the vast diversity of students who are served, a key challenge for student affairs staffs is to define for the community what is meant by student success. Scholars in the field caution that a narrow focus on traditional measures of academic outcomes, such as graduation or transfer rates, will not enable staff to truly assist all students in achieving success. Ender, Chand, and Thornton (1996, p. 45) agree that "For some [success] means transferring to another institution; for others attaining an associate degree, certificate, or additional training; and yet for others it may simply mean gaining confidence in the postsecondary setting or pursuing an interest related to a personal development agenda." In addition, they suggest that student progress and performance be tracked and that students be well informed about their progress toward their goals.

Helfgot (1995, p.33) adds that for community college students, "learning is only a part, albeit a central part, of what it means to be successful.

Success for many [students] is not in learning itself but in the ability to do something with what has been learned." This is a crucial distinction made by several authors in the field who champion the concept of working toward both student learning *and* student success (Ender, Newton, and Caple, 1996).

Proposed Solutions. After examining several exemplary student affairs programs that promote student success at fifty-three community colleges in twenty-three states, Becherer and Becherer (1995) concluded that effective programs have much in common. In their qualitative research, the authors identified several benchmarks of good practice used by student services.

One benchmark addresses the extent to which student services units design programs and services that meet student needs in nontraditional ways. This benchmark suggests that programs and services using new and creative approaches are more likely to be effective in promoting student success than those relying solely on the methods of the past. Some of these approaches include bilingual orientation seminars for ESL students, the use of adaptive technology including synthesized speech and optical pointers that enable a nonverbal individual to engage in spoken dialogue, an on-line new-student orientation program, and a leadership development program that presents students with various programmatic options to learn about and practice leadership.

A second key benchmark involves designing intentional learning experiences for students and encouraging as much student involvement in the planning and implementation of those experiences as is feasible and realistic. Exemplary student affairs programs deliberately encourage and design opportunities for students to be actively engaged in their own learning through a wide variety of peer education programs involving such activities as tutoring, career development, recruitment, orientation, advisement, registration, and special-focus programs that advance student health and wellness. Students who participate learn about teamwork, develop leadership skills, and become valuable resources for their peers at their institutions (Weissman, Bulakowski, and Jumisko, 1998).

A third important benchmark involves student affairs programs that create a sense of belonging between the student and the college. Related to this benchmark, Kuh, Schuh, Whitt, and Associates (1991) discuss the establishment of meaningful bonds between students and their institutions by creating an "ethic of care" across the institution that clearly sends a message to all students that they are individuals who are valued for what they bring to the campus and will be treated with dignity and respect. Exemplary programs include those aimed at assisting students with a variety of special needs to become more integrated into the college and its programs. Special programs and forums in which student concerns and issues can be discussed need to be designed. Promoting an ethic of care and a sense that "all students matter" improves student success by enabling students to identify with their colleges and the various programs and resources available to support them.

A fourth benchmark of exemplary student services emphasizes the need for the development of partnerships between student services and others on and off the campus. Student services professionals need to be proactive in reaching out to other important stakeholders in the community college, especially the faculty, and to collaborate in designing and delivering a wide variety of programs and services for students. This effort could translate into partnerships with students, faculty, instructional support staff, students' families, community leaders, local schools and businesses, and social service agencies. These programs might include teaming with faculty in the classroom by preparing and presenting career modules in courses offered by the faculty or by working to design special activities that support instructional topics addressed by faculty in their classes. Other alliances can also be forged with the community. For example, some student affairs units identify minority leaders representing diverse career fields in the local community and enlist their support to lead seminars on topics related to careers and to serve as role models for students on the campus.

In addition to these four benchmarks described by Becherer and Becherer (1995), student services staff need to take a proactive approach in the delivery of services and programs. Requiring student participation in assessment, advising, orientation, tutoring, and other programs designed to assist in their transition may be advisable, provided that these programs and services are delivered in formats and at times that allow students to participate meaningfully and easily.

Demonstrating Student and Institutional Benefits

One of the primary challenges facing student affairs staffs during the past decade has been the increasing need to demonstrate to key stakeholders the important ways in which student services units support and contribute to an institution's mission. Budget restrictions have forced student affairs staff to move beyond a personal belief in the importance of their work to a more intentional effort both to collect the evidence that demonstrates the programmatic outcomes of student services units and to communicate those findings and their value in enhancing student success to students, faculty, and other administrators (Culp, 1998; Helfgot, 1995).

These calls are part of a larger movement in higher education that demands greater accountability for all institutions. Upcraft and Schuh (1996) stress that all student affairs units in higher education are increasingly being asked to demonstrate to their institutions and regulatory boards that they are delivering on what they promise and doing so in cost-effective and high-quality ways. Resource issues, especially when combined with accountability pressures, often lead institutions to consider reallocating scarce resources to academic priorities, "allocations which are most often narrowly interpreted as support for the faculty, the classroom, the formal curriculum, and those support services that are *clearly* academically related, such as learning support centers and academic advising" (Upcraft and Schuh, 1996, p. 8).

Both Marcus (1999) and Culp (1995) assert that threats to student services programs can arise if a campus culture exists that devalues certain programs and activities for students and if those programs are not seen as central to the institution's survival. Some of these programs may be in "extracurricular" areas (such as student activities, student government, or the arts), as opposed to programs that are more "cocurricular" in focus and perceived as more directly related to academic support and the instructional mission.

Proposed Solutions. The calls for greater accountability in student affairs require increased intentionality about conducting well-designed assessments of programs and services. The community college literature related to student services programs contains numerous recommendations that assessment be conducted but offers little detailed information and few suggestions on just how this can be accomplished on the campus. The absence of practical suggestions for conducting program assessment in the community college student services areas is a serious gap in the literature.

Dungy (1999), however, provides a comprehensive description of the need for research and evaluation in student affairs units in the community college. She states that "serving as a gateway for so many students, community colleges are compelled to study who their students are and to identify barriers between these new students and their ultimate success" (p. 36). Programs and services must be assessed to determine to what extent they are successful and if they need to be changed or ended.

Upcraft and Schuh (1996) are among the few scholars who have focused their attention on assessment issues within student affairs units in higher education. Their six steps to comprehensive assessment involve responding to the following preassessment questions (pp. 25–26): Why are we doing this assessment? What will we assess? How will we assess? Whom will we assess? How will results be analyzed? and How will results be communicated and to whom? The authors provide detailed and helpful information regarding why assessment and evaluation of student affairs programs are critically important as well as excellent overviews of various assessment methods. They also provide practical "how to" examples of assessment in a wide variety of student services program areas.

Finally, while many student affairs professionals recognize the need for and importance of implementing an assessment and evaluation program to respond more effectively to institutional calls for accountability, very few have the training, expertise, experience, or time to design and conduct an effective assessment program. One potential solution is for student services units to establish a good working relationship with institutional research (IR) staff and to support the hiring of an IR staff member who could focus primarily, if not exclusively, on student affairs program assessment. This person could also train student affairs staff to conduct their own studies under the supervision of the IR staff. Dungy (1999) adds that this approach might result in "more decentralization of research across the institution whereby individual units take on some responsibility, with IR serving in a coordinating role to address questions of quality control and support for individuals" (p. 44).

Conclusion

This review of the recent professional literature on student services programs in the community college reveals three broad sets of important challenges professional staff face. First, the increasing numbers and wide-ranging diversity that characterize the primary population served by student services staff raises important challenges and questions about how best to respond to the diverse sets of needs brought to the campus by these students. A second set of challenges arises from the need for student services staff to have a clear and focused mission that will define their work on the campus and that can be communicated across the campus to key stakeholders. Finally, the third set of challenges revolves around the increasing need to demonstrate clearly to key stakeholders the many contributions made both to students and to the institution by student services units and staff.

The review of the literature also reveals that large gaps continue to exist in this literature, especially studies related to the need to respond to increasing calls for accountability by key stakeholders. While several authors consistently recommend that staff conduct assessment, the literature that provides "hands on" and practical examples of quality assessment programs in student services in the community college is scarce. Publications by Schuh and Upcraft (2001; Upcraft and Schuh, 1996) are good resources, but they do not specifically address some of the unique challenges faced in the two-year setting.

In addition, while a wide variety of sources is available that assist student services staff in understanding who their students are and the special needs these students bring to the community college, this review found little in the literature that focuses primarily on noncredit students and how best to address those needs or on the needs of distance education students. These populations of two-year college students are growing and require that staff understand and effectively address their needs as well.

Finally, most recent publications in the field of student affairs administration do not include a focus on the two-year student. This deficiency needs to be addressed—and soon. As Culp and Helfgot (1998) point out, many of the characteristics found among the increasingly diverse community college student population are also being found among students choosing to attend four-year institutions. Student affairs professionals in all institutions of higher education have much to learn from their colleagues who work with students in the two-year sector.

References

American College Personnel Association. *The Student Learning Imperative.* Washington, D.C.: American College Personnel Association, 1996.

Becherer, J. J., and Becherer, J. H. "Programs, Services, and Activities: A Survey of the Community College Landscape." In S. R. Helfgot and M. M. Culp (eds.), *Promoting Student Success in the Community College.* New Directions for Student Services, no. 69. San Francisco: Jossey-Bass, 1995.

Blimling, G. S., and Whitt, E. J. *Good Practice in Student Affairs: Principles to Foster Student Learning.* San Francisco: Jossey-Bass, 1999.

Culp, M. M. "Organizing for Student Success." In S. R. Helfgot and M. M. Culp (eds.), *Promoting Student Success in the Community College.* New Directions for Student Services, no. 69. San Francisco: Jossey-Bass, 1995.

Culp, M. M. "Our Present, Your Future." In M. M. Culp and S. R. Helfgot (eds.), *Life at the Edge of the Wave: Lessons from the Community College.* Washington, D.C.: National Association of Student Personnel Administrators, 1998.

Culp, M. M., and Helfgot, S. R. *Life at the Edge of the Wave: Lessons from the Community College.* Washington, D.C.: National Association of Student Personnel Administrators, 1998.

Dungy, G. J. "View from Community Colleges." In G. D. Malaney (ed.), *Student Affairs Research, Evaluation, and Assessment: Structure and Practice in an Era of Change.* New Directions for Student Services, no. 85. San Francisco: Jossey-Bass, 1999.

Elsner, P. A., and Ames, W. C. "Redirecting Student Services." In G. B. Vaughan and Associates, *Issues for Community College Leaders in a New Era.* San Francisco: Jossey-Bass, 1983.

Ender, K. L., Chand, S., and Thornton, J. S. "Student Affairs in the Community College: Promoting Student Success and Learning." In S. C. Ender, F. B. Newton, and R. B. Caple (eds.), *Contributing to Learning: The Role of Student Affairs.* New Directions for Student Services, no. 75. San Francisco: Jossey-Bass, 1996.

Ender, S. C., Newton, F. B., and Caple, R. B. (eds.). *Contributing to Learning: The Role of Student Affairs.* San Francisco: Jossey-Bass, 1996.

Helfgot, S. R. "Counseling at the Center: High Tech, High Touch." In S. R. Helfgot and M. M. Culp (eds.), *Promoting Student Success in the Community College*, no. 69. San Francisco: Jossey-Bass, 1995.

Helfgot, S. R. "The Student Success Imperative." In M. M. Culp and S. R. Helfgot (eds.), *Life at the Edge of the Wave: Lessons from the Community College.* Washington, D.C.: National Association of Student Personnel Administrators, 1998.

Joint Task Force on Student Learning. *Powerful Partnerships: A Shared Responsibility for Learning.* June 1998 [http://www.aahe.org/assessment/joint.htm].

Kuh, G. D., Schuh, J. H., Whitt, E. J., and Associates. *Involving Colleges: Successful Approaches to Fostering Student Learning and Development Outside the Classroom.* San Francisco: Jossey-Bass, 1991.

Marcus, L. R. "Professional Associations and Student Affairs Policy." *Journal of College Student Development,* 1999, *40*(1), 22–31.

Matson, J. E., and Deegan, W. L. "Revitalizing Student Services." In W. L. Deegan, D. Tillery, and Associates, *Renewing the American Community College: Priorities and Strategies for Effective Leadership.* San Francisco: Jossey-Bass, 1985.

National Center for Education Statistics. *Fall Enrollment in Postsecondary Institutions, 1996.* Washington, D.C.: U.S. Department of Education, 1998.

Ortiz, A. M. "Enhancing Student Development in Community Colleges." *Community College Review,* 1995, *22*(4), 63–70.

Phillippe, K. A., and Patton, M. *National Profile of Community Colleges: Trends and Statistics.* (3rd ed.) Washington, D.C.: Community College Press, 2000.

Rendon, L. I. "Validating Culturally Diverse Students: Toward a New Model of Learning and Student Development." *Innovative Higher Education,* 1994, *19*(1), 33–51.

Schuh, J. H., and Upcraft, M. L. *Assessment Practice in Student Affairs: An Applications Manual.* San Francisco: Jossey-Bass, 2001.

Upcraft, M. L., and Schuh, J. H. *Assessment in Student Affairs: A Guide for Practitioners.* San Francisco: Jossey-Bass, 1996.

Weissman, J., Bulakowski, C., and Jumisko, M. "A Study of White, Black, and Hispanic Students' Transition to a Community College." *Community College Review,* 1998, 26(2), 19–42.

TERRY E. WILLIAMS *is associate professor and chair of the Department of Leadership, Foundations, and Counseling Psychology in the School of Education, Loyola University, Chicago.*

8

In this chapter, the authors identify key challenges for community colleges concerning faculty and professional staff, as identified by consensus or through gaps in the literature: preparing and attracting qualified faculty, implementing the teaching and learning paradigm, helping faculty use current technology, and improving the status and morale of professional staff. For each identified challenge, several potential solutions are proposed.

Community College Faculty and Professional Staff: The Human Resource Challenge

Kim Gibson-Harman, Sandria Rodriguez, Jennifer Grant Haworth

Since the inception of the junior college idea late in the nineteenth century (Rudolph, 1990), community college missions have evolved greatly, as have the perceptions of just what makes up the "community" each should be serving. A diverse cadre of educated professionals is needed to carry out this evolving mission. In addition, some experts would argue that conceptions of community college quality should be gauged not only by student learning outcomes but also by employees' professional growth and their sense of being valued. Indeed, creating a learning environment for both students *and* college employees may well be an additional aspect of the community college's evolving mission. To make better sense of this and other challenges, the discussion in this chapter focuses on literature from the 1990s. The identified challenges and potential solutions make it clear that there is much work to be done for everyone with an investment in the future success of community colleges.

There is considerable consensus that three unfolding developments—a shortage of qualified faculty to meet growing student demand, a movement toward a "learning paradigm" in community colleges, and the pervasive influence of technology—will leave a lasting imprint on a new generation of community college faculty. In addition, professional staff in community colleges—degreed employees who are neither faculty nor administrators—face their own set of unique challenges. This chapter contains descriptions of key developments and challenges for community college faculty and professional staff and outlines predicted challenges and proposed solutions highlighted in recent higher education literature.

A Faculty Shortfall?

A number of scholars have argued that community colleges will experience a significant shortfall in the number of qualified faculty early in the new century (Evelyn, 2001; Keim; 1994; Magner, 2000; McGuire and Price, 1990; O'Banion, 1994).

Predicted Challenges. As root causes of this shortage, several writers (Evelyn, 2001; Keim, 1994; Magner, 2000; McGuire and Price, 1990; Miller, 1997; Milliron and Leach, 1997; Murray, 1999; O'Banion, 1994) present evidence that mass faculty retirements are likely to occur during the first decade of the new millennium, producing unprecedented faculty turnover in community colleges. In addition, these writers warn that undergraduate enrollments could surge as much as 20 percent during this time frame as members of the nation's largest-ever youth cohort enter postsecondary institutions (Howe and Strauss, 2000). The juxtaposition of these two events, argues Miller (1997), presents a serious challenge to community college leaders, who may find themselves hard-pressed to identify talented community college faculty who are adequately prepared to address the needs of an increasingly diverse student population.

Although there is little dispute among scholars that community colleges will be in urgent need of well-prepared faculty as they confront the double-barreled challenges of mass faculty retirements and growing student enrollments, most recognize that various factors may soften the severity of these anticipated shortages. According to Miller (1997), fluctuations in nontraditional student enrollments, institutional budgetary constraints that affect the number of full-time and part-time faculty, the actual reach and incorporation of technology into instruction, and the continued availability of financial aid will all likely influence the "actual need for faculty in community colleges" (p. 88). Higgins, Hawthorne, Cape, and Bell (1995) also stress that despite pending retirements, it is quite likely that a significant number of full-time, tenure-track faculty lines will not be replaced, owing in part to hiring more part-time faculty as a cost-saving measure. Although a recent article by Evelyn (2001) would seem to contradict Higgins and colleagues' forecast that part-time faculty will fill the vacuum left by retiring full-time faculty, their overall point merits attention, particularly since two-thirds of all faculty in public, two-year institutions are employed part time (Banachowski, 1996; Roueche, Roueche, and Milliron, 1995). Recent legislation in some states, however, may limit the growth of part-time faculty in future years, especially if the nation follows California's lead and requires community colleges to adhere to a 75–25 percentage ratio of full-time to part-time faculty (Evelyn, 2001).

If predictions of an impending faculty shortage come true, most scholars concur that recruiting and retaining a well-prepared faculty will present a serious challenge for many community college leaders (Cohen and Brawer, 1996; DeBard, 1995; Grubb, 1999; Miller, 1997; Milliron and Leach, 1997; Murray, 1999). The literature reviewed for this chapter suggests that few graduate programs, let alone community college faculty development initiatives, have seriously addressed the professional development needs of this next generation of faculty. In their classic volume on the community college, Cohen and Brawer (1996) noted that "few community college instructors are prepared in programs especially designed for community college teaching" (p. 78). Miller (1997), in his review of the literature on preservice education and faculty development programs in community colleges, echoed this view, documenting that only a handful of institutions offered coursework or other experiences that prepared master's or doctoral students to teach in community colleges. Of these, none offered a systematic program of study focused on community college teaching.

The literature does offer a few examples of community college–university partnerships that place doctoral students in teaching internships (Magner, 2000; Miller, 1997). While it is probable that there are other preparation initiatives similar to these that have not been reported in the literature, experts agree that graduate institutions have largely failed in their efforts to prepare future faculty for the nation's community colleges (Fugate and Amey, 2000; Grubb, 1999). As Evelyn (2001) reported in the *Chronicle of Higher Education,* "Graduate schools generally don't supply teachers-in-training with the tools they'll need to succeed in the two-year college world. And they don't show any signs of doing so in the near future" (para. 33).

The limited preparation that students receive specifically for community college teaching has led a number of employing institutions to devise faculty development programs, several of which include targeted initiatives for new faculty. According to Outcalt (2000), many of these programs are plagued by nagging problems, including poor planning, limited access and scope, questionable impact, and lack of administrative support. Outcalt's conclusions have been supported by other researchers, many of whom underscore the need to conduct more research on the outcomes of professional development programming on community college faculty (Grubb, 1999; Maxwell and Kazlauskas, 1992; Miller, 1997; Murray, 1999).

Proposed Solutions. Most approaches to dealing with a faculty shortfall emphasize one of three themes: developing and strengthening graduate preparation programs for prospective community college faculty, enriching current faculty development efforts, and recruiting and developing part-time instructors into the ranks of the full-time teaching faculty.

A small number of scholars have discussed the potential of developing community college teaching preparation programs for graduate students. In the early 1990s, for instance, Andrews and Marzano (1990–1991) proposed that apprenticeships or internships become a standard component within any graduate teacher preparation program for community college faculty.

Although she did not advocate the development of graduate preparation programs, Haworth (1999) described efforts currently under way at Princeton University, Michigan State University, and Western Michigan University in which interested graduate students are provided with opportunities to complete "teaching internships" at local community colleges. Grubb (1999) and Miller (1997) have both recommended the development of preservice programs to prepare community college faculty for their teaching responsibilities.

A similarly small group of individuals has sought to enhance current faculty development programs in anticipation of widespread faculty shortages. Perhaps the most consistent theme in the literature has been the need for administrators and faculty to embrace the idea of "one faculty," providing professional development programs that involve full- and part-time faculty in collaborative efforts, often through mentoring programs that pair more experienced full-time faculty with less experienced part-time instructors (Gappa and Leslie, 1997; Roueche, Roueche, and Milliron, 1995). In addition, some individuals have emphasized the need to provide new faculty with a sound understanding of the mission and purpose of community colleges as an important strategy for retaining and enhancing faculty effectiveness. They cite a growing body of evidence that community college faculty who understand and accept the mission of their institutions often hold more positive attitudes toward their work and teach more effectively (DuBois, 1993; Higgins, Hawthorne, Cape, and Bell, 1995).

Finally, a few scholars have suggested that one easy and potentially effective solution to the impending faculty shortage is to "grow your own" through faculty development efforts aimed at part-time faculty (Tsunoda, 1992). The recruitment of full-time practitioners who currently serve as part-time instructors in selected fields—such as business, nursing, and technology—may provide a viable source of future full-time faculty, although there is little evidence in the literature currently to indicate that this is occurring (Parsons, 1992). In fact, despite their comprising 64 percent of the community college faculty workforce (Banachowski, 1996), relatively little attention has been given to part-time faculty since the publication of *Strangers in Their Own Land* (Roueche, Roueche, and Milliron, 1995). Although a certain scholarship developed around the emerging national issue of part-time faculty in the late 1980s and early 1990s, the topic has waned considerably in popularity among community college scholars since then.

The "Learning Paradigm"

While a faculty shortage has just begun to knock on the doors of the nation's community college, a shift to a "learning paradigm" is already under way. This shift has stressed the need to place "learning first in every policy, program, and practice in higher education by overhauling the traditional architecture of education" (O'Banion, 1997, para. 3). Barr and Tagg

(1995) state, "We are shifting to a new paradigm: A college is an institution that exists to produce learning. . . . This shift changes everything" (p. 13).

Predicted Challenges. This shift has created a significant challenge for community colleges, spurring new assumptions about curricular, teaching, learning, and assessment practices in many of them. For instance, Levine (2000) has argued that the learning revolution fundamentally reconceptualizes "how college is taught," emphasizing outcomes- and competency-based frameworks that elevate the centrality of student learning. Other authors have likewise indicated that the learning paradigm has prompted faculty and administrators to adopt competency-based curricula, collaborative and cooperative learning, and technology (such as e-mail, chat groups, and multimedia) as effective strategies for "customizing learning" to the specific needs of a diverse student clientele (Boggs, 1999; Batson and Bass, 1996). Hebel (2000) offers a case in point of this paradigm shift in her profile of Cascadia Community College, a newly opened institution in Bothell, Washington. Designed in light of many of the assumptions that animate the learning paradigm, Cascadia's curriculum is organized around a set of desired learning outcomes, including "thinking critically" and "interacting in diverse and complex environments." Learning communities, interdisciplinary instruction, and team teaching are used as key vehicles for "creating a comprehensive learning environment approach to education" at the college (Hebel, 2000, para. 9).

The emphasis on learning has also challenged educators to become more adept at assessment. Boggs (1999) has written that "perhaps the most important institutional activity for faculty in the learning paradigm is to take the lead in identifying learning outcomes for students and developing ways to ensure that graduates achieve these outcomes" (p. 5). Within this paradigm, student assessment no longer simply means recording a grade on paper and submitting it to the registrar; it is now an integral strategy for gauging and documenting the depth of learning that has occurred in any individual student. Formative rather than summative evaluation methods are employed (Angelo and Cross, 1993; Worthen and Sanders, 1987), as well as performance-based assessment measures (Boggs, 1999; McClenney, 1998).

This gradual but apparent shift from an "instructional" to a "learning" paradigm has prompted many observers to conclude that the roles traditionally performed by faculty are likely to change substantially in the near future (Boggs, 1999; Dickinson, 1999; Levine, 2000; McClenney, 1998; Milliron and Leach, 1997). McClenney (1998) has predicted that the learning revolution will produce "profound changes in the roles of faculty and their relationships to students and one another" since "the traditional model of the lone faculty member lecturing to students sitting in rows in an isolated classroom was never particularly effective educationally . . . [and] is an unaffordable and infeasible model for meeting future demands." Instead, McClenney asserts, faculty in the early twenty-first century will assume new

roles, spending "less time preparing and professing, and more time facilitating reflection, making meaning, and sharing wisdom—managing the process of education" (para. 25).

Boggs (1999) has also argued that the roles played by community college faculty will shift soon, with teachers becoming "responsible for more
important activities than just dispensing information. They will be designers of the learning environment, constantly assessing and seeking improve-
ments" (p. 5). Indeed, there is considerable agreement among scholars that
faculty in the new century will be asked to pay far greater attention to facilitating student learning through their roles as coaches or facilitators
(Cooper, Robinson, and McKinney, 1994), interdisciplinary team members (Ludwig, 2000), brokers of educational experiences (Dickinson,
1999), and cross-disciplinary learning consultants (Milliron and Leach,
1997).

Proposed Solutions. Although several scholars have written about the
learning revolution and its implications for faculty, few have discussed how
community colleges can work with current and future faculty to prepare
them for their new roles as "managers" of student learning.

In the literature reviewed for this chapter, few authors offered strategies for preparing faculty for their changing roles in community colleges.
Of those who did, the solutions presented were broad and general, much
like the list of guiding questions O'Banion (1994) advanced in the early
1990s. Indeed, few concrete solutions have been proposed for tackling the
challenge of preparing community college faculty for their new roles as
"designers of learning environments" (Barr and Tagg, 1995, p. 24), "men-
tors to learners" (Dolence and Norris, 1995, para. 24), and facilitators of
student learning (McClenney, 1998). If a learning revolution is to take firm
root and endure, community college leaders will need to devise creative and
cost-effective strategies to prepare faculty to embrace new professional roles
that few have previously enacted, let alone seen modeled elsewhere.

Faculty Preparation for Technology

Higher education is entering the new millennium on the edge of a "fertile
verge" (Boorstin, 1980), moving from a model of education geared toward
an industrial society to one more appropriate for an information-based
world (Levine, 2000; Paine, 1996). A defining factor in this evolution is
technology. A prevailing idea in the writing on technology and education
in the new millennium is that community college faculty will require new
skills to use the ongoing parade of resources available for effective teaching
and learning (Katz and others, 1999; Keating and Hargitai, 1999; Levine,
2000; Mellander and Mellander, 1999).

Predicted Challenges. One of the greatest thrusts of faculty development at community colleges will need to be centered around faculty preparation for technology-assisted course design and delivery (Carlson, 2000;

Shave, 1998). Although such resources as space, equipment, software, trainers, Web-based course designers, technology training planners, money, and technology support personnel are clearly necessary to prepare faculty effectively for technology-aided instruction (Levin, 1999), an important step may lie in helping instructors make the philosophical shift away from using exclusively traditional approaches to teaching and learning (Alfred, 1998; Katz and others, 1999; Levin, 1999).

Technology training for faculty tends not to be productive unless faculty anxieties about technology are appropriately addressed (Allison and Scott, 1998; Parrott, 1995; Townsend, 1997). For instance, faculty may be concerned about the probability that two dozen packaged on-line courses could replace half of the course requirements at most community colleges (Brown and Duguid, 2000). Such fears may need addressing, as urgently as faculty apprehension about their own technical competency or about the availability of consistent and effective technical support to help with incorporating technology into course design and delivery (Allison and Scott, 1998; Moran and Payne, 1998).

For many community college faculty, often out of step with the demands of educational technology (Dickinson, 1999), philosophical changes regarding course design and delivery may be required. The learning lifestyles of many community college students are steadily becoming entrenched in computer technology prior to their arrival at college (Olsen, 2000; Townsend, 1997). If students are less receptive to faculty lectures that do not incorporate Internet resources and if the majority of freshman students on some college campuses are using the Internet for academic research, then faculty may be compelled to work hard to "keep ahead of the kids" (Olsen, 2000, p. A39). This all points to the idea that faculty roles will have to evolve from teachers to designers of learning experiences, processes, and environments—an evolution that will require a major change in how teachers are prepared and trained (Katz and others, 1999; Keating and Hargitai, 1999).

Proposed Solutions. In addition to the suggestions presented here for helping faculty meet current and future technological challenges, it is also important that administrators encourage faculty to use technology not only as new means of carrying out old tasks but also as tools for conceptualizing and implementing new teaching methods and approaches to expanded learning (Katz and others, 1999). Strong assessment measures of student learning should also be devised, including technology-mediated learning (Brinkley and others, 1999; Katz and others, 1999). Such quality measures can boost the visibility and the marketability of both the college and its students (Carlson, 2000; Carnevale, 2000; Katz and others, 1999). Finally, one proposed solution not described in recent literature certainly merits consideration: incentives in the form of evaluation criteria or job advancement should be provided to faculty, to encourage them to become adept at technology use.

Challenges for Professional Staff

Professional staff members in community colleges are part of a larger body of "support staff" personnel whose ranks have increased tremendously in American higher education over the past twenty-five years. (We use the term *professional staff* to refer to degreed college employees who are not considered faculty, upper-level administrators, or clerical staff.) Grassmuck (1990) indicates that nationwide between 1975 and 1985 alone, there was a 61 percent increase in the number of nonteaching, nonresearch college employees who have jobs that need college degrees. Then, between 1985 and 1990, the percentage of what are termed "middle-level professionals" in academe increased another 28 percent (Grassmuck, 1991). This unparalleled growth in professional staff cannot be ignored by those who seek to make community colleges exciting places of learning and growth for students and for all professional employees.

Predicted Challenges. Professional staff in community colleges will face three key challenges in coming years: status in the organizational hierarchy, morale, and mobility and professional development issues.

Professional status issues and a sense of a lesser "place" are both aspects of community college employee culture and as such play a significant role in defining the work lives of professional staff in community colleges. Intrigued by Gawreluck's study of community college culture (1993), Gibson-Harman (2001) studied master's-prepared professional staff in community colleges, exploring (among other things) professional staff's place in community college culture. By and large, the staff she interviewed found their institutions to be quite hierarchical, with professional staff occupying a place on the ladder somewhat below that of administrators and faculty. Likewise, community college staff members participating in a focus group study conducted by Oudenhoven and Gibson-Harman (1999) reported stratification issues among administrators, faculty, and staff as an area of great concern to them. For many of Gibson-Harman's master's-prepared staff, this was paradoxical, considering their educational credentials, which paralleled those of most faculty in community colleges, and the levels of responsibility and specialized expertise they brought to their work.

Employee perceptions of lesser status on a hierarchy pose another challenge for practitioners because such perceptions often sap staff morale. Low staff morale can have deleterious effects on a college's climate, not only for employees but also for the students. Institutional morale can be assessed by looking not only at "morale" specifically but also at such constructs as campus climate and job satisfaction. Gibson-Harman (2001) found that at some community colleges, the employee group termed "classified staff" spanned a wide range of employees, including specialist staff members with master's or doctoral degrees. Bauer (2000) reviewed literature pertaining to job satisfaction in general and to the job satisfaction of classified staff in higher education institutions in particular. Emphasizing the importance of these staff members as the initial point of contact for many students and their families and the "front line" as far as student services provision is concerned, Bauer identified several factors contributing to classified staff satisfaction on the job: "rewards and recognition, work-life balance, opportunities for growth, training and development, and perceptions of the work environment" (p. 95). She concluded that staff employees who had a sense of being valued would in turn demonstrate greater loyalty and productivity in their work.

The mobility and professional development of professional staff will constitute a key challenge for community colleges in the years to come. As community colleges look to the future, they must be sure to include professional staff in policies and practices related to job mobility and professional development. Bauer (2000) noted that for classified staff in higher education, training and development opportunities did much to enhance job satisfaction, empowerment, and self-esteem. Johnsrud and Rosser (1999, p. 138) found that "perceptions of opportunity and career support" were important to the morale of the mid-level administrators they studied. Likewise, the work of Gibson-Harman (2001) suggests that for professional staff in community colleges, career mobility and professional development were of greater concern to specialist staff than most scholars, administrators, and faculty realize. With recognition of their lesser status on campus, the specialists in her study expressed a desire to somehow improve that status—by promotion, reclassification to a different staff tier, or becoming faculty.

Proposed Solutions. Community colleges can enhance the professional status, morale, and career mobility of their professional staff members in several ways. Regarding staff status, administrators in community colleges should devise ways (such as cross-categorical discussion groups, panels, or focus groups) to engage faculty, staff, and administrators in discussion about their perceptions of employee culture and the messages and interactions that shape these perceptions. Awareness is an important beginning step toward reassessing and changing employee culture (Gibson-Harman, 2001; Oudenhoven and Gibson-Harman, 1999). Also related to status, the sizable pay differentials between faculty and staff with equivalent credentials and experience should be examined and changed to provide greater equity between the two groups (Anderson, Guido-DiBrito, and Morrell, 2000; Gibson-Harman, 2001; Johnsrud and Rosser, 1999).

Community colleges should be sure to acknowledge the professional authority, or authority based on knowledge (Etzioni, 1964), of their specialist staff members and allow them the autonomy in their work that this professional authority implies. Doing this sends a clear message to specialists that they are considered professionals and that their expertise is respected (Gibson-Harman, 2001). The work of professional staff (and other employees as well) needs to be well connected to institutional mission to ensure that these employees feel they have a stake and a role in carrying out the mission (Deal, 1994; Gibson-Harman, 2001).

Finally, the career development and mobility needs of professional staff can be supported in specific ways. Criteria and procedures for movement within staff ranks should be clear and well publicized, and policies should be established *and manifested in practice* allowing for qualified professional staff to be considered for faculty and administrative positions (Gibson-Harman, 2001; Johnsrud and Rosser, 1999; Oudenhoven and Gibson-Harman, 1999). Community colleges should also have professional development incentive programs that reward the achievement of individual goals with pay raises. Linking career development to ongoing learning delivers the message that community colleges value education not only for the constituencies they serve but for their employees as well (Gibson-Harman, 2001; Johnsrud and Rosser, 1999).

Conclusion

The literature reviewed for this chapter suggests that there is both consensus and meaningful omission pertaining to community college faculty and professional staff. The challenges of preparing and attracting faculty to meet the predicted shortages, implementing the teaching and learning paradigm, and helping faculty make effective use of technology have received much attention of late from community college practitioners and scholars. Although the professional staff issues of status, morale, and mobility and professional development may not have received as much attention in print, the literature that does exist indicates that these staff issues merit further research.

Even more important, three overarching themes emerge that connect this body of literature and thought. First, more attention needs to be focused on how faculty and professional staff are prepared for their roles in the community college. Second, once they are part of an institution, their career paths and professional development need nurturing and careful attention. Finally, consideration must be given to what the community college is like as a workplace in this time of rapid change. Is every person a "member of the academy"? What is the culture of each institution, and what defines status and group membership? Are faculty and staff connected to institutional mission? If learning is seen as central to this mission and, as Milliron and Leach (1997) assert, a "learning revolution" is taking place, one can only hope that all the infantry members are being trained, supported, and nurtured enough to want to carry the flag.

References

Alfred, R. "Redesigning Community Colleges to Compete for the Future." *Community College Journal of Research and Practice,* 1998, 22(4), 315–333.

Allison, R., and Scott, D. "Faculty Compensation and Obligation: The Necessity of a New Approach Triggered by Technology Integration." In K. Anandam (ed.), *Integrating*

Technology on Campus: Human Sensibilities and Technical Possibilities. New Directions for Community Colleges, no. 101. San Francisco: Jossey-Bass, 1998.

Anderson, J. E., Guido-DiBrito, F., and Morrell, J. S. "Factors That Influence Satisfaction for Student Affairs Administrators." In L. S. Hagedorn (ed.), *What Contributes to Job Satisfaction Among Faculty and Staff.* New Directions for Institutional Research, no. 105. San Francisco: Jossey Bass, 2000.

Andrews, H. A., and Marzano, W. "Meeting the Looming Faculty Shortage: Development from Within." *Community, Technical, and Junior College Journal,* 1990–1991, *61*(3), 26–29.

Angelo, T. A., and Cross, K. P. *Classroom Assessment Techniques: A Handbook for College Teachers.* (2nd ed.) San Francisco: Jossey Bass, 1993.

Banachowski, G. "Perspectives and Perceptions: A Review of the Literature on the Use of Part-Time Faculty in Community Colleges." 1996. (ED 398 943)

Barr, R., and Tagg, J. "From Teaching to Learning: A New Paradigm for Undergraduate Education." *Change,* 1995, *27*(6), 13–25.

Batson, R., and Bass, R. "Primacy of Process Teaching and Learning in the Computer Age." *Change,* 1996, *28*(2), 42–47.

Bauer, K. W. "The Front Line: Satisfaction of Classified Employees." In L. S. Hagedorn (ed.), *What Contributes to Job Satisfaction Among Faculty and Staff.* New Directions for Institutional Research, no. 105. San Francisco: Jossey Bass, 2000.

Boggs, G. R. "What the Learning Paradigm Means for Faculty." *AAHE Bulletin,* 1999, *51*(5), 3–5.

Boorstin, D. J. "The Fertile Verge: Creativity in the United States." Address given at the Carnegie Symposium on Creativity, the inaugural meeting of the Library of Congress Council of Scholars, Nov. 19–20, 1980.

Brinkley, A., and others. *The Chicago Handbook for Teachers: A Practical Guide to the College Classroom.* Chicago: University of Chicago Press, 1999.

Brown, J. S., and Duguid, P. *The Social Life of Information.* Boston: Harvard Business School Press, 2000.

Carlson, S. "Campus Survey Finds That Adding Technology to Teaching Is a Top Issue." *Chronicle of Higher Education,* Oct. 27, 2000 [http://chronicle. com/chronicle/archive.htm].

Carnevale, D. "Study Assesses What Participants Look for in Higher-Quality Online Courses." *Chronicle of Higher Education,* Oct. 27, 2000 [http://chronicle.com/chronicle/archive.htm].

Cohen, A. M., and Brawer, F. B. *The American Community College.* (3rd ed.) San Francisco: Jossey-Bass, 1996.

Cooper, J. K., Robinson, P., and McKinney, M. "Cooperative Learning in the Classroom." In D. F. Halpern and Associates, *Changing College Classrooms: New Teaching and Learning Strategies for an Increasingly Complex World.* San Francisco: Jossey-Bass, 1994.

Deal, T. E. "The Hidden Agenda: Behind-the-Scenes Employees." *CUPA Journal,* Winter 1994, pp. iii–viii.

DeBard, R. "Preferred Education and Experience of Community College English Faculty: Twenty Years Later." *Community College Review,* 1995, *23*(1), 33–50.

Dickinson, R. "The Changing Role of Community College Faculty: Implications in the Literature." *Community College Review,* 1999, *26*(4), 23–37.

Dolence, M., and Norris, D. *Transforming Higher Education: A Vision for Learning in the 21st Century.* Ann Arbor, Mich.: Society for College and University Planning, 1995.

DuBois, G. "Hidden Characteristics of Effective Community College Teachers." *Community College Journal of Research and Practice,* 1993, *17,* 459–471.

Etzioni, A. *Modern Organizations.* Upper Saddle River, N.J.: Prentice Hall, 1964.

Evelyn, J. "The Hiring Boom in 2-Year Colleges." *Chronicle of Higher Education,* 2001 [http://chronicle. com/chronicle/archive.htm].

Fugate, A. L., and Amey, M. J. "Career Stages of Community College Faculty: A Qualitative Analysis of Their Career Paths, Roles, and Development." *Community College Review,* 2000, *28*(1), 1–22.

Gappa, J. M., and Leslie, D. W. *Two Faculties or One? The Conundrum of Part-Timers in a Bifurcated Work Force.* Washington, D.C.: American Association for Higher Education, 1997.

Gawreluck, R. S. "Organizational Culture in a Community College and Its Interrelationship with Leadership and Structure" Doctoral dissertation, University of Alberta, 1993. *Dissertation Abstracts International,* 1993, *55*(7A), 1760.

Gibson-Harman, K. "The Specialists: Understanding the Work Lives of Master's-Prepared Professional Staff in Community Colleges." Unpublished doctoral dissertation, Loyola University, Chicago, 2001. (ED JC020064)

Grassmuck, K. "Increases in Academic-Support Staffs Prompt Growing Concerns." *Chronicle of Higher Education,* Mar. 28, 1990 [http://chronicle.com/chronicle/archive.htm].

Grassmuck, K. "Colleges Hired More Non-Teaching Staff Than Other Employees Throughout the '80s." *Chronicle of Higher Education,* Aug. 14, 1991 [http://chronicle.com/chronicle/archive.htm].

Grubb, W. N. *Honored but Invisible: An Inside Look at Teaching in Community Colleges.* New York: Routledge, 1999.

Haworth, K. "More Community Colleges Push to Hire Ph.D.'s as Professors." *Chronicle of Higher Education,* Jan. 8, 1999 [http://chronicle. com/chronicle/archive.htm].

Hebel, S. "A Community College Pioneers a Results-Oriented Approach." *Chronicle of Higher Education,* Sept. 15, 2000 [http://chronicle. com/chronicle/archive.htm].

Higgins, C. S., Hawthorne, E. M., Cape, J. A., and Bell, I. "The Successful Community College Instructor: A Profile for Recruitment." *Community College Review,* 1995, *21*(4), 27–36.

Howe, N., and Strauss, W. *Millennials Rising.* New York: Vintage, 2000.

Johnsrud, L. K., and Rosser, V. J. "College and University Midlevel Administrators: Explaining and Improving Their Morale." *Review of Higher Education,* 1999, *22*(2), 121–141.

Katz, R., and others. *Dancing with the Devil: Information Technology and the New Competition in Higher Education.* San Francisco: Jossey-Bass, 1999.

Keating, A. and Hargitai, J. *The Wired Professor: A Guide to Incorporating the World Wide Web in College Instruction.* New York: New York University Press, 1999.

Keim, M. C. "Graduate Preparation Programs in Community College Education." *Community College Review,* 1994, *22*(1), 53–61.

Levin, B. "Distance Learning Close to the Ground." Paper presented at the annual conference of the Southeastern Association for Community College Research, Norfolk, Va., Aug. 1999.

Levine, A. "The Future of Colleges: 9 Inevitable Changes." *Chronicle of Higher Education,* Oct. 27, 2000 [http://chronicle.com/chronicle/archive.htm].

Ludwig, J. "A Web Site Helps Faculty Members Assess Their Instructional Goals." *Chronicle of Higher Education,* Nov. 3, 2000 [http://chronicle.com/chronicle/archive.htm].

Magner, D. K. "The Imminent Surge in Retirements." *Chronicle of Higher Education,* Mar. 17, 2000 [http://chronicle.com/chronicle/archive.htm].

Maxwell, W. E., and Kazlauskas, E. J. "Which Faculty Development Methods Really Work in Community Colleges? A Review of Research." *Community/Junior College Quarterly,* 1992, *16*(1), 351–360.

McClenney, K. M. "Community Colleges Perched at the Millennium: Perspectives on Innovation, Transformation, and Tomorrow." *Leadership Abstracts,* 1998 [http://198.3.183.55/publication/abstracts/leadership/labs0898.html].

McGuire, D., and Price, J. A. "Faculty Replacement Needs for the Next 15 Years: A Simulated Attrition Model." Paper presented at the 29th annual forum of the Association for Institutional Research, Baltimore, May 1990.

Mellander, G., and Mellander, N. "Critical Issues—and Therefore Opportunities—for Community Colleges." Presentation to Congressman Major R. Owens, Congresswoman Carrie P. Meek, the Congressional Progressive Caucus, and the Progressive Challenge. Washington, D.C., July 27, 1999.

Miller, A. A. "ERIC Review—Back to the Future: Preparing Community College Faculty for the New Millennium." *Community College Review,* 1997, 24(4), 83–92.

Milliron, M. D., and Leach, E. R. "Community Colleges Winning Through Innovation: Taking on the Changes and Choices of Leadership in the Twenty-First Century." *Leadership Abstracts,* 1997 [http://198.3.183.55/publication/abstracts/leadership/leadabccwi.htm].

Moran, T., and Payne, M. "Humanizing the Integration of Technology." In K. Anandam (ed.), *Integrating Technology on Campus: Human Sensibilities and Technical Possibilities.* New Directions for Community Colleges, no. 101. San Francisco: Jossey-Bass, 1998.

Murray, J. P. "Faculty Development in a National Sample of Community Colleges." *Community College Review,* 1999, 27(3), 47–64.

O'Banion, T. "Sustaining Innovation in Teaching and Learning." *Leadership Abstracts,* 1994 [http://www.league.org/publication/abstracts/leadership/labs0494.htm].

O'Banion, T. "The Purpose, Process, and Product of the Learning Revolution in the Community College." *Leadership Abstracts,* 1997 [http://www.league.org/publication/abstracts/leadership/labs0797.htm].

Olsen, F. "Campus Newcomers Arrive with More Skill, Better Gear." *Chronicle of Higher Education,* Nov. 2, 2000 [http://chronicle. com/chronicle/archive.htm].

Oudenhoven, D. A., and Gibson-Harman, K. "Reinforcing the Seams: Using Focus Groups to Connect with Specific Employee Groups." Paper presented at a meeting of the Association for Institutional Research, Seattle, June 2, 1999.

Outcalt, C. "ERIC Review: Community College Teaching—Toward Collegiality and Community." *Community College Review,* 2000, 28(2), 57–70.

Paine, N. "The Role of the Community College in the Age of the Internet." *Community College Journal,* 1996, 67(1), 33–37.

Parrott, S. *Future Learning: Distance Education in Community Colleges.* Los Angeles: Clearinghouse for Community Colleges, 1995. (ED 385 311)

Parsons, M. H. "Quo Vadis: Staffing the People's College, 2000." In K. Kroll (ed.), *Maintaining Faculty Excellence.* New Directions for Community Colleges, no. 79. San Francisco: Jossey-Bass, 1992.

Roueche, J. E., Roueche, S. D., and Milliron, M. D. *Strangers in Their Own Land: Part-Time Faculty in American Community Colleges.* Washington, D.C.: Community College Press, 1995.

Rudolph, F. *The American College and University History.* Athens: University of Georgia Press, 1990.

Shave, C. "So You Want to Deliver a Course Using the Internet." Paper contributed to the Teaching in the Community Colleges Online Conference, "Online Instruction: Trends and Issues II," Apr. 7–9, 1998.

Townsend, B. K. "Using the Internet to Teach About the Community College." Paper presented at the annual meeting of the Council of Universities and Colleges, Anaheim, Calif., Apr. 1997.

Tsunoda, J. S. "Expertise and Values: How Relevant Is Preservice Training?" In K. Kroll (ed.), *Maintaining Faculty Excellence.* New Directions for Community Colleges, no. 79. San Francisco: Jossey-Bass, 1992.

Worthen, B. R., and Sanders, J. R. *Educational Evaluation: Alternative Approaches and Practical Guidelines.* New York: Longman, 1987.

KIM GIBSON-HARMAN *is assistant to the campus executive officer at Roosevelt University in Schaumburg, Illinois.*

SANDRIA RODRIGUEZ *is dean of communication arts, humanities, and fine arts at the College of Lake Country, Grayslake, Illinois.*

JENNIFER GRANT HAWORTH *is associate professor in the Department of Educational Leadership, Foundations, and Counseling Psychology at Loyola University, Chicago.*

9

The many governance patterns developed for community college systems reveal the complex relationships states have evolved with these institutions. Policy issues for community colleges demonstrate that these relationships are still in the process of changing.

State Governance Patterns for Community Colleges

Cheryl D. Lovell, Catherine Trouth

Community colleges have shaped the landscape of higher education for one hundred years. The community college system has evolved from one Illinois institution founded in 1901 to over a thousand institutions in 1999 (Tollefson, 2000). This remarkable past has been chronicled from both inside and outside the community college movement. Even with the well-documented history, relatively few discussions have been presented about statewide governance patterns, and even fewer have examined the factors that influence the existing governance systems.

This chapter presents a brief overview of the different types of statewide governance practices and patterns that exist in today's community colleges, followed by a discussion of the factors that influence these statewide governance practices. We then present state and federal policies that affect community colleges at the institutional level and conclude with a discussion of future statewide governance issues.

State Governance Practices, Definition, and Patterns

Community college governance is characterized by a complex web of relationships and arrangements that have evolved over the years. Before specifically examining community college governance structures, it is useful to define the terms used in describing statewide governance. *Governance* is the decision-making authority for an organization, which is typically controlled by boards. Governing boards usually appoint the chief executive of the institution or system, establish policies and approve actions related to faculty and personnel, ensure fiscal integrity, and perform other management functions (Education Commission of the States, 1997).

NEW DIRECTIONS FOR COMMUNITY COLLEGES, no. 117, Spring 2002 © Wiley Periodicals, Inc.

Governing boards are responsible for the specific operation of their institutions or campus systems, but they are only part of the picture of state governance. Statewide coordination is also necessary to ensure that state postsecondary institutions and systems work collectively toward the state interest (Education Commission of the States, 1997). *Statewide coordination* is the formal mechanism that states use to organize higher education. The responsibilities of coordinating boards include statewide planning and policy leadership; defining the mission for each postsecondary institution in the state; academic program review and approval; resource allocation; providing financial aid to students; information, assessment, and accountability systems; and implementing statewide projects (McGuinness, 1997).

Four governing taxonomies have been proposed to help define the many ways in which states have developed statewide organizational structures that apportion governance and coordination responsibilities across institutional types. A brief overview is presented here, but readers wanting a comprehensive discussion should consult the *State Postsecondary Structures Sourcebook,* published by the Education Commission of the States (ECS) (1997).

The first taxonomy classifies states as consolidated governing board states, coordinating governing board states, and planning or service agency states (Education Commission of the States, 1997). Consolidated governing board states assign coordinating responsibilities to a board that also has primary responsibilities to govern the institutions under its jurisdiction. Coordinating board states have boards that serve as coordinating agencies between the state government and the governing boards of the institutions. Governance is decentralized in these states. Finally, planning or service agency states have no statutory entity with coordinating authority but may have an entity to ensure good communication among the institutions or sectors in postsecondary education.

In the second taxonomy, Tollefson (2000) classifies states into five models of state-level coordination and governance similar to the ECS taxonomy. Each state is classified according to which type of state board has responsibility for community colleges. In the first model in Tollefson's taxonomy, the state board of education is responsible for community colleges. This board usually has minimal control, and local boards remain autonomous. In the second model, responsibility for community colleges resides in a state higher education board or commission. In the third model, statewide community college coordinating boards exercise responsibility for community colleges. In the fourth model, there is a state community college governing board with direct control over the community college operations. In the final model, a state board of regents is responsible for community colleges.

The third taxonomy defines statewide structures for all postsecondary institutions in terms of federal systems, unified systems, and segmented systems (Richardson, Baracco, Callan, and Finney, 1998). A federal system organizes institutions under a range of governing boards that are required to work directly with a statewide coordinating board. A unified system places all institutions under a single governing board that works directly with the governor and legislature in budgeting, program planning and approval, articulation, and information collection and reporting. A segmented system has two or more governing boards that supervise single institutions or groups of institutions. In a segmented system, there is no single statewide agency with statutory authority in the areas of budgeting, program planning and approval, articulation, and information collection and reporting.

Building on this third taxonomy, Richardson and de los Santos (2001) suggest a fourth typology: the state community college governance structures typology. This new typology posits seven categories for describing the array of statewide governance systems in place today specifically for community colleges: federal-federal, federal-unified, federal-segmented, unified, segmented-federal, segmented-unified, and segmented-segmented states.

Federal-federal states have local governing boards for colleges, a coordinating board for all higher education institutions, and a separate statewide coordinating structure for community colleges. *Federal-unified states* have one statewide coordinating board for all higher education and a single statewide governing board for community colleges. *Federal-segmented states* have a statewide board that coordinates all higher education and several community colleges or technical institutions that each have their own governing arrangements. *Unified states* have one governing board for all higher education institutions in the state.

Segmented-federal states have two or more governing boards for higher education and either a coordinating board or governing board for community colleges. *Segmented-unified states* have two or more statewide governing boards for higher education, and one of these boards will have responsibility for community colleges. Finally, *segmented-segmented states* have two or more governing boards for higher education, but no board has overall responsibility for community colleges, which in these states are governed by local community college governing boards. These seven categories define the interplay between governing and coordinating boards and the placement of the community college system within the entire higher education community of each state.

Why Model Community College Governance Structures?

These models and taxonomies shed light on the complex relationships states have developed with community colleges. The historical development of community colleges in part explains these complex patterns. Community colleges have been seen at various times as an extension of high school and therefore part of secondary education; as the first two years of a college system; and as a unique educational enterprise separate from both secondary and higher education (Diener, 1994). As the interpretation of the community college changed, governance and coordination patterns also changed, reflecting the move toward placing community colleges firmly in the postsecondary community (Tollefson and Fountain, 1994). Governance patterns continue to change as the definition of the community college evolves.

By understanding governance and coordination systems, leaders can anticipate strengths and weaknesses of the systems for meeting future challenges. For instance, where statewide boards supervise both two- and four-year colleges, two-year colleges are often overlooked by board members, who concentrate on what they perceive as more pressing issues at the four-year institutions. Yet these systems may be well positioned to respond to demands for improved articulation and collaboration in a K–16 postsecondary model (Richardson and de los Santos, 2001).

These taxonomies also help define the placement of community colleges within a state system. Depending on its place in the state system, a community college may face many levels of governance and coordination, which can create problems. Conflicts between state and local boards or between boards and the state legislature can arise when there is a dispute or some ambiguity over which entity has governing responsibilities. The existence of multiple levels of governance may also contribute to these misunderstandings about responsibilities. For example, a recent California study found that twenty-two different agencies and offices shared community college governance responsibilities (Davis, 2001).

Factors Influencing Statewide Governance

Several factors affect statewide governance systems for community colleges today. The most important factors include board composition, articulation issues, and collective bargaining agreements.

Board Composition. Board composition has far-reaching consequences for a community college. Studies conducted on boards of trustees for all types of institutions show that governing board members are usually white, over age fifty, and male, although women and minorities are represented on governing boards of public institutions in slightly greater proportions than on those of private institutions (Hines, 1997). The ethnic and gender composition of boards often do not reflect the diverse constituencies they serve, though the question remains open as to how this affects policy decisions or whether the symbolism of a board's composition influences decisions such as students' choosing to enroll or taxpayers' willingness to support the institution.

Members of both governing and coordinating boards can be appointed or elected. Popular election is practiced for local community college boards in at least twenty states (Hines, 1997). One might assume that board members elected by popular vote might legitimately represent the interests of diverse stakeholders, but with low voter turnouts at some elections, it might be easier for special-interest groups to influence the outcome of the election (Davis, 2001).

At public institutions in which board members are appointed, the governor usually makes the appointments. Board agendas may change whenever a new political party wins the governor's office. Sometimes the appointment of a single board member can lead to an abrupt change in direction for the institution (Davis, 2001). Davis suggests that irresponsible board members should be subject to recall, whether they are appointed or elected. A well-designed provision for recall that protects good members from attacks for unpopular decisions would encourage board members to hold themselves to high standards of governance.

Articulation Issues. One of the oldest missions of community colleges is to provide the first two years of education for students seeking a bachelor's degree (Rifkin, 1998). States have approached articulation between community colleges and other institutions in different ways. Most states have promoted voluntary articulation agreements, meaning that institutions are encouraged to negotiate agreements among themselves. Other states have legislated policies that enhance articulation, such as a common course-numbering system or a core general education curriculum (Rifkin, 1998). Voluntary articulation agreements put this governance issue in the hands of local boards, while legislative policies place this issue in the hands of state-level boards.

Recently, Illinois created a new means of articulation through the Illinois Articulation Initiative (IAI). This initiative created a statewide general education core curriculum as well as several model lower-division curricula in a number of majors. Faculty panels from public and private two-year and four-year institutions review course syllabi from participating institutions to determine which institutional courses are "equivalent to," and therefore satisfy, the IAI general education or major-specific courses (Rifkin, 1998). The IAI approach makes articulation a joint concern of both community college and higher education boards at the state level.

Collective Bargaining Agreements. Collective bargaining agreements, which may exist at the college or statewide level, have important effects on governance. The statewide agreements—those encompassing all community colleges in the state—have considerable influence over governance systems. Unions represent 51 percent of full-time faculty at public two-year institutions and 27 percent of part-time faculty (National Center for Education Statistics, 2001). Many of these agreements can limit the span of management control of governing or coordinating boards as the issues are decided in the contract negotiations rather than at the board level.

State and Federal Policies

Since both federal and state policies affect community colleges, governing boards must be aware of the effect of these policies and work with both state and federal governments to shape policies that further the goals of their institutions. Three areas of particular interest are federal financial aid, workforce preparation, and state funding.

Federal Financial Aid. Probably one of the most important federal influences on American higher education is the federal financial aid program. Federal financial aid regulations raise issues for community colleges that other institutions do not face (Lovell, 2001). For example, in many states, community colleges provide the bulk of remediation for students. Since federal regulations limit the amount of financial aid that may be used for remedial coursework, campus administrators must monitor course-taking patterns of students on a larger scale than baccalaureate institutions (Lovell, 2001). There are also ability-to-benefit (ATB) requirements in place that pertain to institutions with open access. Open access is one of the primary characteristics of community colleges, so these requirements have a particularly large impact on these institutions. These requirements are in place to ensure that a student receiving federal financial aid has the potential to successfully complete a program, which places additional monitoring and reporting constraints on participating institutions. A final area of concern for community colleges is that federal financial aid policies limit aid to part-time students. This is a critical issue for community colleges because many of their students attend on a part-time basis.

Workforce Preparation. Recent federal legislation created a number of federal and state school-to-work and vocational preparation programs. The Workforce Investment Act and the reauthorized Perkins Vocational Act were passed in 1998. These legislative acts tied federal funding to workforce training offered on campuses and were intended to build a competitive workforce (Lovell, 2001). Workforce preparation is already one of the primary goals of community colleges. Federal funding regulations and state interpretations of federal legislation, as they pertain to federal funds that flow through states to individual institutions, shape and influence how local institutions develop and deliver their programs. Workforce preparation funding requires state-wide governance vigilance, as stewardship of these preparation measures is necessary to ensure adequate support programs for citizens in the state. As Debra Bragg discusses in Chapter Three, little is yet known about the actual impact of many federal workforce preparation initiatives.

State Funding. While community colleges in many states still collect support through local taxes, usually property taxes, the trend for the past three decades has been for states to fund an increasing percentage of community college operating costs (Education Commission of the States, 2000). This raises the question as to whether there will then be a shift away from local governance control toward greater state governance or coordination for community colleges. One study found that while the authority resided with the state boards, much of that authority was delegated to local community colleges (Tollefson, 1996). Community colleges have so far retained much of their local governance control, but there is no guarantee that states will continue to delegate their authority to the local boards.

Emerging Issues for Statewide Governance and Policy

As noted, community colleges have just recently celebrated their hundredth year as part of America's higher education system. As they prepare for their next hundred years, several policy issues will challenge those who govern community colleges.

Changing Statewide Structures for Community College Governance and Coordination. From 1963 to 1989, major changes in the types of state-level boards for community colleges occurred, including an increase from thirty-eight to forty-nine states with statewide community college systems and an increase from six to twenty-two states with separate state boards specifically for community colleges (Tollefson, 1996). While there have not been as many changes in statewide governance structures since 1989, a number of states have recently considered such changes. Florida provides the most prominent example of reorganization. In 2000, the Florida legislature eliminated most of the state's postsecondary boards, including the state's Board of Community Colleges, in favor of one board of education for the entire school system in Florida. The purpose of this reorganization is to redefine the educational system in Florida as one seamless K–20 system. Since the change will not be completed until 2003, it is not yet clear how this change will affect the community colleges in the state.

Other states in the process of reviewing their statewide governance systems for postsecondary education are Arizona, California, Colorado, Iowa, Pennsylvania, and West Virginia. Changes are usually intended to improve the effectiveness and responsiveness of state systems. For example, in Iowa, legislators introduced a bill to establish a task force to study the restructuring of governance in order to make community colleges run more cooperatively, effectively, and efficiently as a state system. In Colorado, a report from the Northwest Education Research Center recommended that Colorado consider certain structural realignments in its governance system to increase the potential for responsiveness to community and regional higher education needs.

Seamless K–16 System. Many states are calling for a seamless K–16 educational system to better prepare and serve their citizens and the states' needs. Creating such systems could have far-reaching consequences for the governance of community colleges. The integration of K–12 and postsecondary systems may require states to reconsider the traditional separation of K–12 and higher education governance (Boswell, 2000). Florida's education reorganization eliminates this separation. In three other states, Ohio, Maryland, and Georgia, higher education board members at both the local and state levels are working on K–16 councils aimed at establishing reform (Boswell, 2000).

Technology. As access to technology increases, students may choose a community college on the basis of cost and range of offerings rather than geographical proximity (Mingle and Ruppert, 1998). This could profoundly affect community colleges, which are dependent on attracting students from the local geographical area. For example, in 1997, Colorado created the Colorado Community College Online, a collaborative effort to offer degrees from thirteen community colleges and one university on the Internet (Mingle and Ruppert, 1998). The interconnection of a state's community colleges on-line may increase the trend away from local governance and toward greater state governance and coordination. As the geographical boundaries of community colleges erode, it is harder to define the constituency of the college and therefore harder to establish a governing body that reflects that constituency.

Redefining the community college mission is also a potential concern to statewide governance. Some leaders have discussed possible transformations of the role of community colleges, such as transforming community colleges into four-year colleges or changing them into two-year university branch campuses. The current literature is contradictory, weak, or inconclusive regarding the extent to which the mission of community colleges should be redefined; some have called for recasting the community college as a noncollegiate institution concerned primarily with vocational education. If the mission of community colleges changes, then changes in statewide systems for coordination and governance will be required as well. Yet the literature is also contradictory about what constitutes an appropriate model of governance for community colleges. What seems most evident is that multiple models exist, there is no single "best" model, and patterns of governance are shaped by multiple influences related to all levels of education and to state-specific issues and politics.

Conclusion

Community college governance has undergone tremendous changes in the past hundred years. As community colleges enter their second century, they face issues that will continue to redefine their place in the American educational system. These changes seem to be redefining community colleges more as state-level than local institutions. Community college leaders often need training in facing these changes and in understanding their relationship to various constituents, including the state.

Many organizations provide support for these leaders. The Association of Community College Trustees provides trustee education and assists boards in developing and affecting public policy. The American Association of Community Colleges also provides information on legislation affecting community colleges and actively promotes the goals of community colleges in Washington, D.C. The Education Commission of the States recently established the Center for Community College Policy to conduct research on policy issues affecting community colleges and to organize workshops on the issues community colleges face.

Local board members, faculty, and staff at community colleges should be proactive in reviewing state systems. They need to ensure that states carefully consider the purposes of community colleges before deciding on system changes. At the same time, community college leaders will want to understand the legitimate needs of the state in helping to coordinate their institutions. This means understanding the whole system of statewide coordination and understanding where their particular institution belongs in this system.

References

Boswell, K. "Building Bridges, Not Barriers: Public Policies That Support Seamless K–16 Education." In Center for Community College Policy (ed.), *Community College Policy Handbook*. Denver: Education Commission of the States, 2000.

Davis, G. "Issues in Community College Governance." Issue paper for "New Expeditions: Charting the Second Century of Community Colleges," an A W. K. Kellogg Foundation Initiative sponsored by the American Association of Community Colleges and the Association of Community College Trustees. 2001 [http://www.aacc.nche.edu/intitiatives/newexpeditions/White_Papers/governancewhite.htm]

Diener, T. "Growth of an American Invention: From Junior to Community College." In J. L. Ratcliff, S. Schwarz, and L. Ebbers (eds.), *Community Colleges*. (2nd ed.) Boston: Allyn & Bacon, 1994.

Education Commission of the States. *State Postsecondary Structures Sourcebook: State Coordinating and Governing Boards*. Denver: Education Commission of the States, 1997.

Education Commission of the States. *State Funding for Community Colleges: A 50-State Survey*. Denver: Education Commission of the States, 2000.

Hines, E. R. "State Leadership in Higher Education." In L. F. Goodchild, C. D. Lovell, E. R. Hines, and J. I. Gill (eds.), *Public Policy and Higher Education*. Boston: Allyn & Bacon, 1997.

Lovell, C. D. "Federal Policies and Community Colleges: A Mix of Federal and Local Influences." In B. K. Townsend and S. B. Twombly (eds.), *Educational Policy in the 21st Century*, Vol. 2: *Community Colleges: Policy in the Future Context*. Westport, Conn.: Ablex, 2001.

McGuinness, A. "The Function and Evolution of State Coordination and Governance in Postsecondary Education." In Education Commission of the States. *State Postsecondary Structures Sourcebook: State Coordinating and Governing Boards*. Denver: Education Commission of the States, 1997.

Mingle, J. R., and Ruppert, S. S. "Technology Planning: State and System Issues." In Center for Community College Policy, *Community College Policy Handbook*. Denver: Education Commission of the States, 1998.

National Center for Education Statistics. *Institutional Policies and Practices: Results from the 1999 National Study of Postsecondary Faculty, Institution Survey*. Washington, D.C.: U.S. Department of Education, 2001.

Richardson, R., and de los Santos, G. "Statewide Governance Structures and Two-Year Colleges." In B. K. Townsend and S. B. Twombly (eds.), *Educational Policy in the 21st Century*, Vol. 2: *Community Colleges: Policy in the Future Context*. Westport, Conn.: Ablex, 2001.

Richardson, R. C., Baracco, K. R., Callan, P. M., and Finney, J. E. *Designing State Higher Education Systems for a New Century*. Westport, Conn.: Oryx Press, 1998.

Rifkin, T. "Improving Articulation Policy to Increase Transfer." In Center for Community College Policy, *Community College Policy Handbook*. Denver: Education Commission of the States, 1998.

Tollefson, T. A. "Emerging Patterns in State-Level Community College Governance: A Status Report." 1996. (ED 437 076)

Tollefson, T. A. "Martorana's Legacy: Research on State Systems of Community Colleges." Paper presented at the annual meeting of the Council for the Study of Community Colleges, Washington, D.C., Apr. 2000. (ED 443 461)

Tollefson, T. A., and Fountain, B. E. In J. L. Ratcliff, S. Schwarz, and L. Ebbers (eds.), *Community Colleges*. (2nd ed.) Boston: Allyn & Bacon, 1994.

CHERYL D. LOVELL *is associate professor of higher education and adult studies at the University of Denver. In the past, she has worked for the National Center for Higher Education Management Systems and the State Higher Education Executive Officers.*

CATHERINE TROUTH *is a doctoral student in higher education and adult studies at the University of Denver. She has recently worked on policy projects with the Western Interstate Commission for Higher Education and the Education Commission of the States.*

10

Practitioners and scholars have available a vast array of publications about community colleges, but it is not always easy to determine which are the most important or most timely. This chapter provides a list of literature that the contributors to this issue of New Directions for Community Colleges deem key to the subjects covered in their chapters.

Key Literature

This chapter provides an annotated bibliography of the literature that the authors of this issue of *New Directions for Community Colleges* feel are of key importance to the subjects covered by their chapters. The authors were asked to select four to six publications. Most focus on community colleges; some take a broader perspective but are of significant value to community colleges. Taken as a whole, the authors' recommendations comprise a reading list that will be useful to practitioners who seek to gain a general knowledge of community colleges, to graduate students and faculty in courses about the community college, to trustees who want to learn about community colleges in general, and to librarians and professional development specialists building a collection of resources about community colleges.

Transfer

Grubb, "The Decline of Community College Transfer Rates: Evidence from National Longitudinal Surveys" (1991), illustrates how data from national studies (National Longitudinal Surveys, High School and Beyond Surveys) can give insight into community college transfer rates and baccalaureate attainment. Although the data are now more than fifteen years old, the article provides a useful national picture of some transfer patterns during the 1970s and 1980s.

Adelman, *Answers in the Tool Box: Academic Intensity, Attendance Patterns, and Bachelor's Degree Attainment* (1999), is a more recent example of the use of national databases, along with high school and college transcripts and test scores, to study baccalaureate attainment, including transfer students. The report is significant for its documenting of some major trends in college attendance patterns as well as degree completion.

De los Santos and Wright, "Maricopa's Swirling Students: Earning One-Third of Arizona State's Bachelor's Degrees" (1990), is important for being one of the first articles to describe and document (in laypersons' language) the complexity of student transfer patterns. The authors coin the term *swirling* to describe students' movement "between and among community colleges and four-year institutions on the way to the baccalaureate" (p. 32) and give evidence of this phenomenon for students attending Maricopa Community College.

Illinois Community College Board, *Calculating Transfer Rates: Examining Two National Models in Illinois* (1994), provides a comparative overview of two models that have been used to determine transfer rates at the national level: the model used by the Center for the Study of Community Colleges (CSCC) and that used by the National Effectiveness Transfer Consortium (NETC). ICCB used both models to determine the transfer rate for an entering cohort (CSCC model) and an exiting cohort (NETC model with some modifications). The report is useful not only for its close examination of these two models but also for clearly showing how transfer rates differ, depending on the numerator and denominator used in calculating the percentage of transferring students.

Vocational Education

Boesel and McFarland, *National Assessment of Vocational Education, Final Report to Congress* (1994), provides a comprehensive evaluation of vocational programs in the United States. Until subsequent NAVE reports are released later this year, this report presents the most current information we have on the status of vocational education following implementation of new federal legislation on vocational education in 1990.

The fall 2001 issue of *New Directions for Community Colleges,* on the "new vocationalism," edited by Bragg, provides chapters concerning reform of vocational education in community colleges in the United States. Leading scholars and practitioners in the field, including W. Norton Grubb, Margaret Terry Orr, Carrie Brown, and James Jacobs, provide valuable insights concerning how vocational education is changing in community colleges and how new ideas and models are replacing old ways of doing business. The authors report numerous changes that are intended to more fully integrate and articulate vocational education with other aspects of the postsecondary curriculum.

Grubb, *Working in the Middle: Strengthening Education and Training for the Mid-Skilled Labor Force* (1996), provides an in-depth understanding of subbaccalaureate vocational education programs directed at the technical occupations in the United States. The text addresses economic changes that have influenced workforce patterns, new vocational curricular offerings in community colleges, and the outcomes of postsecondary vocational programs directed at students who use community and technical colleges to prepare for jobs in the U.S. technical workforce.

Grubb and others, *Workforce, Economic, and Community Development: The Changing Landscape of the Entrepreneurial Community College* (1997), summarizes the new role of community colleges with respect to the non-traditional workforce and economic and community development. The authors define new roles for the community college as part of an "entre-preneurial college," and they review trends and issues related to these efforts. The report also presents recommendations for promoting and inte-grating the notion of entrepreneurial colleges into other community col-leges.

Hershey, Silverberg, Owens, and Hulsey, *Focus for the Future* (1998), reports on the results of the national evaluation of tech prep. It describes how tech prep was implemented through 1995 and identifies implementa-tion practices and challenges. This report is the most recent published account of tech prep implementation in all tech prep consortia in the nation.

Remedial Education

The Winter 1997 issue of *New Directions for Community Colleges* edited by Ignash, *Implementing Effective Policies for Remedial and Developmental Education,* has a specific focus on community colleges and is a good start-ing place for understanding who needs remedial education and why, costs associated with remediation, and measures of effectiveness. Each chapter addresses a specific policy question, sometimes by exploring state and national policies and sometimes by highlighting a particular case study.

McCabe, *No One to Waste: A Report to Public Decision-Makers and Community College Leaders* (2000), offers a comprehensive overview of social issues and trends, provides a broad context for understanding the issues related to remediation, and includes recommendations to public deci-sion makers and community college leaders for the future.

Phipps, *College Remediation: What It Is, What It Costs, What's at Stake* (1998), was written in the aftermath of the City University of New York's decision to phase out remediation at CUNY's four-year colleges and limit community college remediation to one year. The report examines purposes, participants, financial costs, social and economic consequences, and strate-gies for the future. The author concludes that remediation is a core func-tion of higher education.

Roueche and Roueche, *High Stakes, High Performance: Making Remedial Education Work* (1999), is a commissioned study by the American Association of Community Colleges. The authors seek to organize current information and focus discussion about remedial education for educators, policymakers, the media, and the public.

The National Center for Developmental Education (NCDE) Web site (http://www.ced.appstate.edu/centers/ncde) and National Association of Developmental Education (NADE) Web site (http://www.umkc.edu/cad/nade) offer access to many helpful articles and publications, including the writings of

Dr. Hunter R. Boylan, the director of NCDE. These sites provide a "whole person" developmental perspective, going beyond the remediation of skills deficiencies.

English as a Second Language

Harklau, Siegal, and Losey, *Generation 1.5 Meets College Composition: Issues in the Teaching of Writing to U.S.-Educated Learners of ESL* (1999), is the premier text for issues affecting Generation 1.5 students, much of it applicable to the community college setting.

Four journals are of particular interest in the ESL area. *TESOL Quarterly* is a scholarly journal focusing on both linguistic research and pedagogy, while *TESOL Matters* deals more with the political and practical state of the profession. *Teaching English in the Two-Year College,* though not specifically about ESL, often includes articles on community college ESL, with both a research and classroom focus. The *Journal of Second Language Writing* also contains valuable information for community college ESL practitioners and researchers.

Kuo, "English as a Second Language in the Community College Curriculum" (1999), presents an excellent overview of the state of ESL at the community college.

The community college ESL listserv (eslcc@hcc.Hawaii.edu) is a valuable resource, especially with respect to professional and employment concerns.

Assessment

Alfred, Ewell, Hudgins, and McClenney, *Core Indicators of Effectiveness for Community Colleges* (1999), provides a concise but relatively comprehensive review of the major indexes of institutional effectiveness for community colleges.

Banta, *Assessment Update: The First Ten Years* (1999), is a compendium of ten years' worth of articles and columns by some of the top national authorities on assessment from *Assessment Update,* the bimonthly assessment journal-newsletter from Jossey-Bass.

Borden and Owens, *Measuring Quality: Choosing Among Surveys and Other Assessments of College Quality* (2001), is a comprehensive description of available standardized surveys and tests that may be used as components of an overall model to assess institutional effectiveness and student learning outcomes.

Doucette and Hughes, *Assessing Institutional Effectiveness in Community Colleges* (1990), although now more than ten years old, remains the single best source for comprehensive information and practical guidance on assessment in community colleges.

Gardiner, Anderson, and Cambridge, *Learning Through Assessment: A Resource Guide for Higher Education* (1997), presents a comprehensive overview of the assessment literature, associations, and organizations dealing with assessment, assessment conferences, assessment instruments, and Internet and multimedia resources available regarding assessment.

Student Services

Culp and Helfgot, *Life at the Edge of the Wave: Lessons from the Community College* (1998), will be helpful for anyone working with students in institutions of higher education on both two-year and four-year campuses. The authors provide a fresh new perspective on the unique needs of new generations of students arriving on campus and on how institutional support programs can best respond. Staff in four-year institutions can benefit from the lessons learned about students and their success in the community college.

The issue of *New Directions for Student Services* that Helfgot and Culp edited in 1995, *Promoting Student Success in the Community College*, addresses similar topics to those in Culp and Helfgot (1998). However, this monograph focuses on the key roles served in the community college by student services professionals.

Upcraft and Schuh, *Assessment in Student Affairs: A Guide for Practitioners* (1996), provides a thoughtful and comprehensive primer for student affairs staff desiring to conduct program evaluations in a wide variety of student services units on campus. It should be consulted in conjunction with the authors' recently published handbook, cited next.

Schuh and Upcraft, *Assessment Practice in Student Affairs: An Applications Manual* (2001), is a comprehensive manual that provides excellent practical suggestions and advice for conducting a wide range of assessments in student affairs programs.

Faculty and Professional Staff

Grubb and Associates, *Honored but Invisible: An Inside Look at Teaching in Community Colleges* (1999), is excellent reading for community college faculty and administrators. Grubb and his colleagues carefully examine the state and quality of teaching in American community colleges. Their conclusions, based on interviews and classroom observations of 257 community college instructors in thirty-two community colleges in eleven states, highlight the lack of attention given to preparing faculty for the demands of community college teaching, as well as the lack of institutional support provided to support teaching and professional development in the nation's teaching colleges.

Johnsrud and Rosser, "College and University Midlevel Administrators: Explaining and Improving Their Morale" (1999), and Johnsrud, Heck, and Rosser, "Morale Matters: Midlevel Administrators and Their Intent to Leave"

(2000), are important resources for researchers interested in exploring staff morale issues.

Katz and others, *Dancing with the Devil: Information Technology and the New Competition in Higher Education* (1999), examines the increasing role of technology in higher education. Specifically addressed are strategies for competing with other education providers, promoting innovation in technology, developing needed structural and administrative flexibility, and financing technological change.

Governance

Center for Community College Policy, *Community College Policy Handbook* (2000), is a collection of policy papers on issues community colleges face, including articulation, K–16 education, and technology issues for states and state systems. The center plans to add new policy papers to the handbook as they are written. The handbook is available at http://communitycollege policy.org.

Cohen and Brawer, *The American Community College* (1996), is a comprehensive review of community colleges in the United States, including an analysis of the utility of community colleges in today's postsecondary environment. The authors provide a critical review of enrollment trends, employment practices, curricular offerings, and technology influences.

Tollefson, Garrett, Ingram, and Associates, *Fifty State Systems of Community Colleges: Mission, Governance, Funding, and Accountability* (1999), includes data on trends in governance, finance, educational assessment, accountability, and economic development. They also discuss models of state-level coordination and governance that emerged by the late 1990s.

Townsend and Twombly, *Community Colleges: Policy in the Future Context* (2001), compiles papers that discuss policies affecting community colleges in the future, including federal policies, accountability, K–14 education, state policies and the community college's role in workforce preparation, and statewide transfer and articulation policies. The book also includes the Richardson and de los Santos conceptual model of state structures for community colleges.

References

Adelman, C. *Answers in the Tool Box: Academic Intensity, Attendance Patterns, and Bachelor's Degree Attainment.* Washington, D.C.: Office of Educational Research and Improvement, U.S. Department of Education, 1999.

Alfred, R., Ewell, P., Hudgins, J., and McClenney, K. *Core Indicators of Effectiveness for Community Colleges.* (2nd ed.) Washington, D.C.: Community College Press, 1999.

Banta, T. W. (ed.). *Assessment Update: The First Ten Years.* Boulder, Colo.: National Center for Higher Education Management Systems, 1999.

Boesel, D., and McFarland, L. *National Assessment of Vocational Education: Final Report to Congress,* Vol. 1: *Summary and Conclusions.* Washington, D.C.: Office of Educational Research and Improvement, U.S. Department of Education, 1994.

Borden, V.M.H., and Owens, J.L.Z. *Measuring Quality: Choosing Among Surveys and Other Assessments of College Quality.* Washington, D.C.: American Council on Education, 2001.

Bragg, D. D. "Opportunities and Challenges for the New Vocationalism in American Community Colleges." In D. D. Bragg (ed.), *The New Vocationalism in American Community Colleges.* New Directions for Community Colleges, no. 115. San Francisco: Jossey-Bass, 2001.

Center for Community College Policy. *Community College Policy Handbook.* Denver: Education Commission of the States, 2000.

Cohen, A. M., and Brawer, F. B. *The American Community College.* (3rd ed.) San Francisco: Jossey-Bass, 1996.

Culp, M. M., and Helfgot, S. R. *Life at the Edge of the Wave: Lessons from the Community College.* Washington, D.C.: National Association of Student Personnel Administrators, 1998.

de los Santos, A. G., and Wright, I. "Maricopa's Swirling Students: Earning One-Third of Arizona State's Bachelor's Degrees," *AACJC Journal,* 1990, *60*(6), 32–34.

Doucette, D., and Hughes, B. (eds.). *Assessing Institutional Effectiveness in Community Colleges.* Laguna Hills, Calif.: League for Innovation in the Community College, 1990.

Gardiner, L. F., Anderson, C., and Cambridge, B. L. (eds.). *Learning Through Assessment: A Resource Guide for Higher Education.* Washington, D.C.: American Association for Higher Education, 1997.

Grubb, W. N. "The Decline of Community College Transfer Rates: Evidence from National Longitudinal Surveys." *Journal of Higher Education,* 1991, *62*(2), 194–222.

Grubb, W. N. *Working in the Middle: Strengthening Education and Training for the Mid-Skilled Labor Force.* San Francisco: Jossey-Bass, 1996.

Grubb, W. N., and Associates. *Honored but Invisible: An Inside Look at Teaching in Community Colleges.* New York: Routledge, 1999.

Grubb, W. N., and others. *Workforce, Economic, and Community Development: The Changing Landscape of the Entrepreneurial Community College.* Mission Viejo, Calif.: League for Innovation in the Community College, 1997.

Harklau, L., Siegal, M., and Losey, K. M. (eds.). *Generation 1.5 Meets College Composition: Issues in the Teaching of Writing to U.S.-Educated Learners of ESL.* Mahwah, N.J.: Erlbaum, 1999.

Helfgot, S. R., and Culp, M. M. (eds.). *Promoting Student Success in the Community College.* New Directions for Student Services, no. 69. San Francisco: Jossey-Bass, 1995.

Hershey, A. M., Silverberg, M. K., Owens, T., and Hulsey, L. K. *Focus for the Future: The Final Report of the National Tech Prep Evaluation.* Princeton, N.J.: Mathematica Policy Research, 1998.

Ignash, J.M. (ed.). *Implementing Effective Policies for Remedial and Developmental Education.* New Directions for Community Colleges, no. 100. San Francisco: Jossey-Bass, 1997.

Illinois Community College Board. *Calculating Transfer Rates: Examining Two National Models in Illinois.* Springfield: Illinois Community College Board, 1994.

Johnsrud, L. K., and Rosser, V. J. "College and University Midlevel Administrators: Explaining and Improving Their Morale." *Review of Higher Education,* 1999, *22*(2), 121–141.

Johnsrud, L. K., Heck, R. H., and Rosser, V. J. "Morale Matters: Midlevel Administrators and Their Intent to Leave." *Journal of Higher Education,* 2000, *71*(1), 34–59.

Katz, R., and others. *Dancing with the Devil: Information Technology and the New Competition in Higher Education.* San Francisco: Jossey-Bass, 1999.

Kuo, E. "English as a Second Language in the Community College Curriculum." In G. Schuyler (ed.), *Trends in Community College Curriculum.* New Directions for Community Colleges, no. 108. San Francisco: Jossey-Bass, 1999.

McCabe, R. H. *No One to Waste: A Report to Public Decision-Makers and Community College Leaders.* Washington, D.C.: Community College Press, 2000.

Phipps, R. *College Remediation: What It Is, What It Costs, What's at Stake*. Washington, D.C.: Institute for Higher Education Policy, 1998.

Roueche, J. E., and Roueche, S. D. *High Stakes, High Performance: Making Remedial Education Work*. Washington, D.C.: Community College Press, 1999.

Schuh, J. H., and Upcraft, M. L. *Assessment Practice in Student Affairs: An Applications Manual*. San Francisco: Jossey-Bass, 2001.

Tollefson, T. A., Garrett, R. L., Ingram, W. G., and Associates. *Fifty State Systems of Community Colleges: Mission, Governance, Funding, and Accountability*. Johnson City, Tenn.: Overmountain Press, 1999.

Townsend, B. K., and Twombly, S. B. (eds.). *Educational Policy in the 21st Century*, Vol. 2: *Community Colleges: Policy in the Future Context*. Westport, Conn.: Ablex, 2001.

Upcraft, M. L., and Schuh, J. H. *Assessment in Student Affairs: A Guide for Practitioners*. San Francisco: Jossey-Bass, 1996.

INDEX

Students: diversity of, 68–69; ESL (English as a second language) needs of, 45; federal financial aid and, 96; four worker groups of vocational, 27; Generation 1.5, 49–51; inconsistent standards/policies applied to, 37–38; remediation and, 35–43; "swirling" phenomenon and, 20; transfer, 13, 15–18, 57–58; vocational program overrepresentation by African American, 28; vocational/workforce training programs for, 25–32, 96; as WIA (Workforce Investment Act) recipients, 25–26, 27. *See also* Assessing learning outcomes

STWOA (School-to-Work Opportunities Act) [1994], 29, 30

"Swirling" phenomenon, 20

Szelényi, K., 18

Tagg, J., 80, 82

Tech prep/school-to-work transition programs, 29

Technology: predicted challenges of using new, 82–83; proposed solutions of learning new, 83; as statewide governance issue, 97–98

Terenzini, P. T., 61

Theses research literature, 7–8

Thornton, J. S., 68, 70

Tichenor, S., 48

Tinto, V., 14

TOEFL scores, 37, 46

Tollefson, T. A., 91, 92, 94, 96, 97, 106

Townsend, B. K., 1, 13, 23, 30, 31, 41, 83

Traditional occupational/technical vocational programs, 27–28

Transfer Assembly Project (2001), 18

Transfer Assembly Project of the Center for the Study of Community Colleges, 14

Transfer students: definitional issues in determining, 15–18; falling rate of, 13; learning outcomes of, 57–58; literature on, 101–102. *See also* Community college transfer rates

Transfer/applied baccalaureate programs, 15, 30–31. *See also* Community college transfer rates

Transitional workers/workforce, 27

Trinkle, K. A., 30

Trouth, C., 2, 91, 100

Truman College (Chicago), 47

Tsunoda, J. S., 80

Twombly, S. B., 106

Unified states governing boards, 93

Upcraft, M. L., 72, 73, 74, 105

Utility purpose of literature, 9

Valiga, M. J., 26, 31, 55

Vocational program research: on for-credit/noncredit workforce training, 31; on school-to-work/work-based learning, 29–30; on tech prep/school-to-work transition, 29; on traditional occupational/technical, 27–28; on transfer/applied baccalaureate, 30–31

Vocational programs: four worker groups of students in, 27; future directions of, 31–32; growth of, 25–26, 96; literature on, 102–103; overrepresentation of African Americans in, 28; recent changes in, 26–27; research on curricula of, 27–32

Walleri, R. D., 59, 60

Warford, L., 27

Watson, B. C., 39, 41, 42

Watson-Glaser Critical Thinking Appraisal, 56

WBL (work-based learning), 30

"Weekend Social Science Option," 56

Weiler, D., 17

Weissman, J., 39, 40, 71

Western Michigan University, 80

Whitt, E. J., 70, 71

WIA (Workforce Investment Act), 25, 26

William Rainey Harper College (Illinois), 50–51

Williams, T. E., 2, 67, 76

Workforce training programs, 31, 96. *See also* Vocational programs

Wright, I., 20, 102

Zimbler, L., 27

Back Issue/Subscription Order Form

Copy or detach and send to:

Jossey-Bass, A Wiley Company, 989 Market Street, San Francisco CA 94103-1741

Call or fax tollfree: Phone 888-378-2537 6AM-5PM PST; Fax 800-605-2665

Back issues: Please send me the following issues at $28 each.

(Important: please include series initials and issue number, such as CC114)

1. CC _____

_____

_____

$ _____Total for single issues

$ _____ SHIPPING CHARGES: SURFACE

	Domestic	Canadian
First Item	$5.00	$6.50
Each Add'l Item	$3.00	$3.00

For next-day and second-day delivery rates, call the number listed above.

Subscriptions: Please ❏ start ❏ renew my subscription to *New Directions for Community Colleges* for the year 2____ at the following rate:

U.S.	❏ Individual $66	❏ Institutional $135
Canada	❏ Individual $66	❏ Institutional $175
All Others	❏ Individual $90	❏ Institutional $209

$ _____Total single issues and subscriptions (Add appropriate sales tax for your state for single issue orders. No sales tax for U.S. subscriptions. Canadian residents, add GST for subscriptions and single issues.)

Federal Tax ID 135593032   GST 89102 8052

❏ Payment enclosed (U.S. check or money order only)

❏ VISA, MC, AmEx, Discover Card # _____ Exp. date_____

Signature _____ Day phone _____

❏ Bill me (U.S. institutional orders only. Purchase order required)

Purchase order #_____

Name _____

Address _____

_____

Phone_____ E-mail _____

For more information about Jossey-Bass, visit our Web site at: www.josseybass.com

PROMOTION CODE = ND3

CC105 Preparing Department Chairs for Their Leadership Roles
Rosemary Gillett-Karam
Presents the qualities that experienced department chairs cite as being
crucial to success and makes a persuasive argument for the need to develop
formal training programs for people newly appointed to these positions.
ISBN: 0-7879-4846-2

CC104 Determining the Economic Benefits of Attending Community College
Jorge R. Sanchez, Frankie Santos Laanan
Discusses various state initiatives that look at student outcomes and
institutional accountability efforts and analyzes the trend to connect
accountability and outcome measures with funding.
ISBN: 0-7879-4237-5

**CC103 Creating and Benefiting from Institutional Collaboration: Models for
Success**
Dennis McGrath
Examines the many ways collaboration both benefits and alters the
participating organizations, offering practical examples and lessons learned
that can be used by a variety of institutions in their efforts to foster
collaborative relationships.
ISBN: 0-7879-4236-7

**CC102 Organizational Change in the Community College: A Ripple or a Sea
Change?**
John Stewart Levin
Presents real-life examples of community colleges' experiences with
organizational change—both successful and unsuccessful—and examines
organizational change through a variety of theoretical frameworks, including
feminism and postmodernism.
ISBN: 0-7879-4235-9

**CC101 Integrating Technology on Campus: Human Sensibilities and Technical
Possibilities**
Kamala Anandam
Addresses the topics of organizational structures, comprehensive economic
planning, innovative policies and procedures, faculty development, and
above all, collaborative approaches to achieving significant and enduring
results from technological applications.
ISBN: 0-7879-4234-0

**CC100 Implementing Effective Policies for Remedial and Developmental
Education**
Jan M. Ignash
Addresses specific policy questions involved in the debate over remedial and
developmental education and uses national and state data, as well as
information from case studies of individual institutions, to provide insights
into effective approaches to remedial and developmental education.
ISBN: 0-7879-9843-5

CC99   Building a Working Policy for Distance Education
Connie L. Dillon, Rosa Cintron

Presents some of the policy issues confronting higher education in the age of distance learning, and discusses the implications of these issues for the community college.
ISBN: 0-7879-9842-7

CC98   **Presidents and Trustees in Partnership: New Roles and Leadership Challenges**
Iris M. Weisman, George B. Vaughan
Explores the professional needs, challenges, and roles of community college governing board members and their presidents—and how these factors influence the board-president team.
ISBN: 0-7879-9818-4

CC97   **School-to-Work Systems: The Role of Community Colleges in Preparing Students and Facilitating Transitions**
Edgar I. Farmer, Cassy B. Key
Demonstrates how community colleges are engaged in strengthening existing partnerships with schools, employers, and labor- and community-based organizations as they develop new programs to address the three major components of school-to-work systems.
ISBN: 0-7879-9817-6

CC96   **Transfer and Articulation: Improving Policies to Meet New Needs**
Tronie Rifkin
Presents recommendations for current and future transfer and articulation policies in an attempt to expand the discourse and thereby enhance the ability of community colleges to serve their own educational goals as well as the educational goals of this nation.
ISBN: 0-7879-9893-1

CC95   **Graduate and Continuing Education for Community College Leaders: What It Means Today**
James C. Palmer, Stephen G. Katsinas
Provides critical perspectives on the current status of community college education as an academic specialty.
ISBN: 0-7879-9892-3

CC89   **Gender and Power in the Community College**
Barbara K. Townsend
Examines the gender socialization that results in stereotypes that usually operate to women's disadvantage socially, politically, and economically and explores ways the community college experience can be structured to overcome this disadvantage.
ISBN: 0-7879-9913-X

CC77   **Critical Thinking: Educational Imperative**
Cynthia A. Barnes
Considers ways in which high-level thinking skills can be integrated with content and taught across institutional disciplines and means by which instructors and administrators can become involved in these efforts.
ISBN: 1-55542-749-9